The Consumer's Journey *to* **_Purchasing_** Funeral Services

A Marketing Roadmap for Growing Market Share and Revenue

BILL A JOHNSTON

ISBN: 978-0-9972745-7-8 (paperback)
ISBN: 978-0-9972745-8-5 (eBook)
ISBN: 978-0-9972745-9-2 (Audio book)

Library of Congress Control Number: 2024906390

Printed in Daphne, Alabama by Bill A Johnston

Photo credits
Book Cover Image from iStock ID: 107007232 Licensed to Bill A Johnston February 2, 2024
Book cover design by Nathan Dasco
Headshots by Jennifer Ayer

This book is not intended for use as a source of legal, business, accounting, or financial advice. All readers are advised to seek the services of competent professionals in legal, business, accounting, and financial fields.

The advice and strategies found within may not be suitable for every situation. This work is sold with the understanding that neither the author nor the publisher is held responsible for the results accrued from the advice in this book.

The author has strived to be as accurate and complete as possible in the creation of this book. While all attempts have been made to verify information provided for this publication, the publisher assumes no responsibility for errors, omissions, or contrary interpretation of the subject matter herein.

The author is intentionally not using any Meta Brand Assets. Throughout the book the author will estimate data elements associated with the performance of a paid or sponsored post. They are only estimates and not actual results as a part of any ad campaign purchased by Post and Boost, Inc., or its customers.

For more information, visit www.PostandBoost.com.

Table of Contents

INTRODUCTION

Are you seeing your cremation percentage going up and your cash flow percentage going down? You're not alone. The entire funeral industry is seeing it, a shift in consumer preferences exacerbated by the COVID-19 pandemic, and it's not going away. Nope. It's going to keep growing. That's why the alarm bells are going off. Change is in the air.

If you decide you are going to bring a change to your business, and change means growing market share and revenue, then this marketing and advertising book for funeral homes is for you. It is written from the perspective of "brand" advertising. As we enter Chapter 13, How Advertising Works, we will make the distinction between brand advertising and direct marketing so there is complete clarity.

Now if the exact answers you are seeking are not found here, that's okay. This book is a thought starter. Whether you're a marketing and advertising Leader, an Essentialist, or anywhere in between, there's something in this book that will benefit everyone. And I believe while you're reading it, there will be something in this book for you, too. As thoughts and ideas begin to cross your mind, *your* answers will come forth. I am excited to help you discover them. To make sure you remember them, write then down directly in the book.

This book begins by painting a picture of an imaginary journey by a consumer who will someday purchase funeral services. It's how they're first exposed to death and the funeral process through the lens of marketing and advertising. You'll see how their thinking progresses as they live their life and how their mind can be influenced by advertising as they get closer to the moment of purchase. Your objective? To visualize the consumer's journey to purchasing funeral services. If you can see it, then you have gained the insights you need to effectively connect to them so that, when they decide to buy, when they call, click, or show up at the front door, your funeral home is the only and obvious choice.

A little about me. My perspective, where I'm coming from, is as a former broadcaster of 25 years and business owner for more than 20 years. I've worked with hundreds of direct retail advertisers and written thousands of ads. Some ads and advertising campaigns were successful, while others could have been better. I also have a deep background in sales, sales management, mastering the complex sales process, and technology.

Today, I own an interactive software and advertising production company, Post and Boost, Inc., a leading provider of Facebook advertising for funeral homes. I'm also a speaker, a certified provider of continuing education in multiple states, and author of four books including my last book, *How Facebook Works for Funeral Homes*.

Now I totally get how some funeral homes don't have a lot of time for the topic of marketing and advertising. Creating marketing and writing advertising for funeral homes is not exactly easy, but having been in the industry since 2016, I have figured out some things you would be interested to know. For example, when I first started posting and boosting on Facebook for Jim and Paula Lowe at Lowe Funeral Home and Crematory in Burlington NC, I asked a lot of questions. The question that got me the biggest and most important answer was, "What makes your funeral home unique?" Jim quickly responded. "It's our people. Our people make us unique."

After listening to Jim and Paula, I started to take pictures of people. People standing in foyers, next to lecterns, in visitation rooms, chapels, or in front of the building. I combined these pictures with written copy in posts about "death and the funeral process." That's not exactly a topic you learn about in college (I graduated from the Newhouse School of Communications at Syracuse University with a degree in Television and Radio in 1977). Nope. And it's not a topic you learn to write about from funeral professionals. Most I talk to and post and boost for are quick to tell me they don't know what to say in advertising or social media. They tell me, "You're the expert." When it comes to advertising and what to say, I guess I am.

Yes, I do know what to say. That's another thing I figured out. I have plenty of experience writing copy for retail customers in broadcasting. When I met Ven Faulk, Owner and Funeral Director at Shumate Faulk Funeral Home and Crematory, Goldsboro NC, that was the first time I began writing ads for funeral homes. Many of the words I use today came from long conversations with Ven. When I decided to become a Facebook expert, he was my first client. I'm thankful to him for that.

What I have learned along the way is how advertising works, and that means knowing how to structure advertising campaigns to get results for my clients. As you enter the roadmap portion of this book, you'll learn what I learned about The Four Pillars of Effective Local Advertising. It's a clear, commonsense way to approach advertising that can be applied to any media.

And if I have figured out anything that is big for our industry, my aha moment, is that the consumer has the answers. By listening to the consumer and hearing what their needs are, what their dreams are, what they are thinking, and how they come to make purchases that are influenced by marketing and advertising designed to change the way they think, that's where I'm coming from. It was collaborating with Jim and Paula where I was allowed to take pictures of people and write ads that educated the consumer on death and the funeral process.

It was what we saw on Facebook during my early days of posting and boosting for the Lowe Funeral Home & Crematory Facebook page that has become the guiding principle in our business, Post and Boost, Inc. We saw first-hand how consumers organically reacted to real people on Facebook. It was as natural as a perfectly controlled focus group. Consumers were engaging in our Facebook advertising, and commenting on staff members with the kind of celebration and recognition that can only be given to special, compassionate people. It was very positive, and if you were a customer of mine at Post and Boost®, it would be positive for you, too.

That's the answer. The consumer told us that real people on Facebook work. It's also the reason we feature people on radio and television ads. As Jim Lowe said, "our people make us unique." As I give credit to the consumer and how they interact with our advertising on Facebook, I can confidently say *what I think or what you think is not nearly as important as what a consumer thinks*, and we heard them loud and clear.

But just like how every consumer is different, we know every funeral home is different, too. Chapter 9 looks at Funeral Home Types, and what will become clear in that chapter is not every funeral home's marketing and advertising can be based on the people who represent your brand. It's why I will ask you these two questions throughout the book: "Do you know who you are, and do you know what you stand for?"

In the first half of this book, you will understand why and when a consumer would watch, listen, read, or purposefully remember your advertising. As we enter "The Consumer's Journey to Purchasing Funeral Services" you'll discover the five phases of the Funeral Sales Funnel. As we progress, you'll uncover how to categorize consumers into "Funeral Buyer Types," and then as you think about your marketing and your advertising, your Funeral Home Type, and how you will "match" them together. Chapter 10, What Makes a Funeral Home Unique, introduces the concept of how funeral homes create "tension" in the mind of a new consumer. It also prepares you for Chapter 18, Educating the Consumer, which explains how education can be used as the forward motion to relieve that tension.

You see, the funeral consumer has a problem, and it's the biggest problem they will ever face. The problem is death. Either their pending death or the death of someone they hold close. Seth Godin, in his book *This is Marketing: You Can't Be Seen Until You Learn to See*, said, "Marketing is the generous act of helping someone solve a problem. *Their problem*" (Godin, 2018). Let's help them do that.

Throughout this book I will reference Seth Godin. To give his words the kind of weight they deserve in the world of marketing and advertising, I would compare him to someone you may know. Todd Van Beck was to the funeral industry what Seth Godin is to the world of marketing – a towering figure whose influence shaped perspectives and set new benchmarks for excellence. Just as Van Beck transformed the funeral industry with his profound understanding of funeral service practices, education, and compassionate care, Godin has revolutionized marketing with his insights into consumer behavior, branding, and storytelling. I sincerely hope drawing parallels between these two influential figures can bridge the gap between marketing theory and practical application within your business.

The second half of the book is the roadmap. It's my roadmap for you. Yes, there are others that work, but my hypothesis, my reveal, is how we break down the consumer, how they think, the uniqueness of a funeral home and the market it serves. Then we apply effective marketing and advertising principles in ways I believe can work for you. I also introduce, "The Informative Advertising Style," featuring real people providing valuable information to consumers traveling through The Consumer's Journey of Purchasing Funeral Services using a variety of media. From marketing ideas like events and ceremonies, to advertising strategies on Meta Platforms (Facebook, Instagram) and mass media, this roadmap can get you where you want to go. Do all these things in a certain way and put yourself in the position to grow your market share and revenue.

The idea for this book came from a conversation with NFDA's Sara Moss. We were talking about what title I should give my new seminar going in to 2024. When I mentioned a part of our most recent seminar, "Busting the Myths of Local Advertising for Funeral Homes," and the segment where we describe the consumer's journey to purchasing funeral services, she reacted to it. She liked it. And after talking with Diana M. Needham, my long-time mastermind partner who is also an amazing business book marketing expert, we both loved the title, and agreed it would be a good book to write.

Hope you like it!

Reader's Guide: "How to Navigate This Book"

Welcome to "The Consumer's Journey to Purchasing Funeral Services." Before you dive into the chapters that lie ahead, I'd like to offer some guidance on how to navigate this book so that you get the most out of it.

In Chapter 3, there are three marketing and advertising "styles." In Chapters 3-7, there are the five phases of the consumer's journey. Chapter 8, "Funeral Buyer Types," details four buyer types, each with multiple personas, and then it's followed by Chapter 9, "Funeral Home Types," where there are six funeral home types. What you may discover is, after you have finished Part I, given the detailed categorizations and the breadth of topics covered, it might be challenging to remember them all, and you'll want to for this book to achieve its intended purpose for you.

To make it easy, I'm going to list them out here:

The Three Marketing and Advertising Styles as detailed in Chapter 3

1. **Leader**. A "Leader" consistently employs innovative marketing and advertising strategies that set their funeral home apart.
2. **Aspirant**. Being an "Aspirant" means there's a strong desire to enhance marketing and advertising, yet often finds itself constrained by time, resources, or knowledge.

3. **Essentialist**. An "Essentialist" tends to focus on tradition, is heavily reliant on "word-of-mouth," and will resist marketing and advertising.

The Five Phases of The Consumer's Journey to Purchasing Funeral Services as detailed in Chapters 3-7

1. **Awareness**. When a consumer becomes aware of the need for funeral services.

2. **Interest.** When a consumer has a growing level of curiosity and passive need for more information.

3. **Desire.** When a consumer has been triggered by a significant event or shocking information.

4. **Action.** A consumer calls, clicks, or comes through your front door.

5. **Retention**. They've been served before, or they have pre-planned with you. What you are doing to keep them as future customers.

The Four Funeral Buyer Types as detailed in Chapter 8

1. **The Immediate, "Ad-Need" Buyer**. Buyers prepared to purchase services immediately because someone has died, or death is imminent.

2. **The Preplanner**. Preplanners are buying for themselves or a loved one.

3. **The Price Sensitive Buyer**. When price is the issue, it's the only issue.

4. **The Customizer**. A buyer most interested in personalizing services that reflect the unique life of the deceased.

The Six Funeral Home Types as detailed in Chapter 9

1. **The Premier Funeral Home.** Leads in market share. Perceptually the most trusted.
2. **The Emerging Funeral Home.** New to the market, an established firm with new leadership or recently purchased.
3. **The Plateaued Funeral Home.** The status quo is a guide. Appears to be stable but is slowly losing market share.
4. **The Innovator Funeral Home.** Incorporates modern, non-traditional services. Forward thinking.
5. **The Price Strategy Funeral Home.** Advertising a low price. Direct cremation fits here, too.
6. **The Specialty Funeral Home.** This is a funeral home that focuses on a specific religious, ethnic, or cultural service.

As you read through the book you can always come back to this Reader's Guide. And a key thought: Throughout the book I will continually ask if you know who you are and what you stand for. If you take a pen to this Reader's Guide and circle your marketing and advertising style, circle the Funeral Buyer Type you are most interested in, and circle your Funeral Home Type, you may have answered the question.

Another resource at the end of the book, called Reference 2, lists a group of powerful worksheets designed to help you work through some of the concepts we are presenting to you. Worksheets have a way of organically structuring learning, makes self-assessments easier, and bridges the gap between abstract concepts and practical implementation.

One final idea if you want: Read Chapter 8 (Funeral Buyer Types) and Chapter 9 (Funeral Home Types) first, then return to Chapter 1. When you return to Chapters 8 and 9, reading them again will enhance your comprehension of the rest of the book.

PART I

Understanding the Consumer's Journey, Buyer Types, and Funeral Home Types

CHAPTER ONE

"Why Would a Consumer Watch, Listen, Read, or Purposefully Remember An Ad For a Funeral Home?"

How many ads does the American consumer get exposed to in a day? 100? 500? According to the Forbes article, "Finding Brand Success in the Digital World" by Jon Simpson (Simpson, 2017), it's around 4,000 to 10,000 ads a day. Whoa! If a consumer is exposed to thousands of ads a day, how does a local retail advertiser like your funeral home "break through"?

Yes, you're a *retail* advertiser. Business to consumer. B2C. Think about it. Where did today's funeral home get its start? From the mid-1800s through the early 1900s, it was in a furniture store. As cabinet makers made caskets, and employees discovered a second income as "undertakers," the funeral industry began to organically grow.

Local and regional historians in towns and counties across America have written about this aspect of funeral history. Here's an example: The Hillsdale County Historical Society (Hillsdale, MI) online article titled, "Funeral Sales and Funeral Homes" (Lackey, Unknown). It reads, "One of the earliest undertakers in Hillsdale was William Donaghy, who in 1874 advertised, 'Wholesale and Retail Dealer in Coffins, Caskets, and all kinds of Undertaker's trimmings, shrouds, etc.' at No. 4 Farnum's Block on Broad Street." If that sounded like local, retail advertising for a furniture store, it was.

Some funeral homes would love to have that freedom of advertising like a furniture store, or maybe creating retail ads that are different, something that "breaks through." They could be funny instead of morbid. Just search YouTube "Funeral Home TV Ads," and watch the classic, fictional WKRP Ferryman Funeral Home clip. The staff sings a jingle that says, *"Hey! You're young and swingin.' No time to think about tomorrow. But there ain't no way to deny it. Someday you're gonna buy it. So plan today for a Ferryman, tomorrow!"* Outside the sound booth, the President of Ferryman Funeral Homes is bouncing to the beat with glee. Hilarious! The ad ends with WKRP's Johnny Fever delivering the tag: *"Six...count 'em. Six convenient locations, plus group rates and free parking. It's all yours at Ferryman Funeral Homes."* (Hugh Wilson, 1979)

If you continue with that YouTube search, you'll also see real funeral home commercials. Some are well produced; others are obviously locally made. Some are funny, and I'm sure the funeral homes who made them got plenty of feedback. But is it the kind of feedback *you* want? Does a funeral ad based on comedy or a gimmick that "breaks through" unintentionally alienate a significant group of consumers who believe final moments and memories for themselves or a loved one should be based on something else besides a catchy commercial or cute Facebook post?

"Funeral services aren't sold like recliners or sofas."

Pure, retail advertising feels uncomfortable or inappropriate in the context of funeral services. That's because funeral services are not sold like recliners or sofas, let alone trumpeted with comedy that interrupts the flow of daily life or the consumer's personal moments. It's a delicate balancing act. How do you respect the sensitive emotions surrounding death, while at the same time make an invitation to purchase funeral services?

That's a challenge for funeral homes today. It isn't easy writing ads about death and the funeral process. I mean, what do you say? And when you combine that with now knowing consumers see so many ads every day, _why_ would anyone want or need to watch, listen, read, or purposefully remember an ad for a funeral home? It feels like it won't work. And besides, everyone knows a funeral home's best form of advertising is "word of mouth." Right?

Yes. "Word of mouth" is *the* most effective form of advertising. It's also slow and expensive, expensive because it *is* slow. If you have the patience, the time, and the years to expand your business based on that singular "Essentialist" approach, you can. It's a roadmap. Many have done it and have been successful.

But if you're reading this book to grow your market share and revenue sooner, this is my roadmap for you. It's based on doing things in a certain way using The Informative Advertising Style described later in the book. It combines an advertising style consistent with your profession, strategies that leverage current market and media conditions, and your funeral home's reputation by using real people.

The goal is simple: to close the gap. To shorten the number of years it takes to amplify revenue and multiply profits. When you have more cash flow, you can do more. Pay for your kid's college, live in a nicer home, liberally give to causes and charities you're passionate about. Or maybe you'd like to hire more people to work for you so you can take a vacation, grow into more locations, or position your business to be sold at a premium price. Whatever the reason, if you feel you deserve more, I agree with you.

The Funeral Sales Funnel

In the next chapter you'll see a picture of the Funeral Sales Funnel that has been customized for funeral services. It's helps you visualize the five phases consumers may go through on their Journey to Purchasing Funeral Services. You'll follow them from the time they become aware of funeral services, to being interested, to having the desire to purchase funeral services based on a need, and ultimately making a purchase by taking action. Action can represent anything from clicking a link and filling out a form, to making a phone call or physically walking through your doors.

Why Would a Consumer Watch, Listen, Read, or Purposefully Remember an Ad For a Funeral Home?

Now, to answer the question why would a consumer begin to watch, listen, read, or purposefully remember your advertising. As you'll read in the upcoming chapter called Desire – The Third Phase of the Consumer's Journey, something has happened in their life, a trigger or significant moment that caused a transition.

It could be they were told they have six months to live, or a loved one will die soon, so you can imagine the range of responses like shock, anger, or depression. The reality is the consumer has a problem. It's the biggest problem they will ever face.

The first thoughts of a pending death can have a profound effect on a consumer. It's a new state of heightened emotional sensitivity that dominates and permeates their mind. If the consumer's mind is dominated by this problem, the reality of death, and if death and the funeral process is all they can think about, then their mind will be "On" for your advertising. It's then they will actively watch, listen, read, or purposefully remember your advertising. The On Phenomenon (see Reference 1) is a comprehensive explanation as to why. It describes the Baader-Meinhof Phenomenon, and "Why do we keep noticing certain things more often?" (Henderson, 2023) It's this part of their journey when funeral home marketing and advertising perceptually begins being noticed.

> *"Marketing is the generous act of helping someone solve a problem. Their problem." – Seth Godin*

Seth Godin, in his book *This is Marketing: You Can't Be Seen Until You Learn to See*, said, "Marketing is the generous act of helping someone solve a problem. *Their problem*" (Godin, 2018). This perspective frames marketing and advertising as compassionate outreach – offering solutions, answers, and forward momentum to consumers. Depending on the age of the consumer and what is happening in their life and the lives of their loved ones, the

Journey to Purchasing Funeral Services could take days, months, years, or decades. We're all different and we all have different needs, and in most cases, death is not predictable. This variability underscores the importance of maintaining consistent marketing efforts. Consistency ensures that when a need arises, often unexpectedly, your funeral home is the only and obvious choice.

The Marketing Roadmap

The second half of this book, the marketing roadmap for growing market share and revenue, will explain the four ways to grow your business, how marketing and advertising works, and introduce you to The Informative Advertising Style. It's a marketing and advertising style using real people that can match your Funeral Home Type and Marketing and Advertising Style.

To narrate my intended result for you as an objective or mission statement, my change for you would be:

"To professionally, consistently, and effectively market to Ideal Consumers in a certain way for the purpose of establishing an equity position in their mind, so that when they consciously decide to purchase funeral services, your firm is top of mind, making it the only and obvious choice."

Let's discover the foundation of The Consumer's Journey to Purchasing Funeral Services by introducing you to the Funeral Sales Funnel. That's next.

Key Thoughts from Chapter 1:

1. The average consumer sees around 4,000 to 10,000 ads a day.

2. Funeral Homes are retail, business to consumer, advertisers.

3. Word of mouth is the most effective form of advertising. It's also slow and expensive.

4. The journey to purchasing funeral services could take days, months, years, or decades. It's why consistency in your marketing is vitally important.

5. If the consumer's mind is dominated by this problem, the reality of death, and if death and the funeral process is all they can think about, then their mind will be "On" for your advertising.

6. Consumers who are "On" for funeral services will begin to actively watch, listen, read, or purposefully remember funeral service advertising.

7. Marketing and advertising for funeral homes can be framed as compassionate outreach.

The Funeral Sales Funnel

Awareness

Interest

Desire

Action

Retention

CHAPTER TWO

The Funeral Sales Funnel

How can you visualize a consumer on their journey to purchasing funeral services? It begins with a picture of the Funeral Sales Funnel. The theory of a "funnel" in marketing and advertising is an accepted, visual metaphor. As a graphic, the sales funnel is a useful and visual representation that depicts the "flow" of potential customers through the different phases of a decision-making process, from initial awareness to the final action of purchasing. It's shaped like a funnel, with a wide top and narrow bottom, to represent the gradual decrease in the number of potential consumers at each phase of the process.

The purpose of a sales funnel as a graphic is to provide a visual representation of the different phases of decision making. By understanding the flow, marketing and advertising can be targeted so that resources are used more efficiently, and there's a framework for measuring results, performance, or conversion.

The sales funnel is versatile because it can be applied across a broad spectrum of business-to-business and business-to-consumer businesses, from high-value items like cars and homes, to everyday consumer goods like gasoline, sub sandwiches, and hamburgers. The phases are Awareness, Interest, Desire, Action, and Retention. You've probably heard of the acronym for this, "AIDA" or "AIDAR," where the "R" is for retention or sometimes recall. And despite the differences in products, price points, or purchasing frequency, the phases for any business type remain relatively the same.

What's important to recognize is as consumers age out (or become deceased), new ones come in. The funnel is an ongoing cycle. That means your marketing and advertising efforts are continuous, with no definitive endpoint.

The Funeral Sales Funnel

Perceptually, funeral services are a big-ticket item. Not bigger than a car or a house, but being in the $5,000 - $25,000 range, it's still a big ticket, one-time purchase (with future purchases, if applicable, within the retention phase). That's why I am painting a big ticket, marketing sales funnel so that you can visualize the consumer's "journey" from the top to the bottom.

The top of the Funeral Sales Funnel is the widest, and the bottom, compared to other businesses, is going to be very small, almost tiny. That's because there's a finite number of consumers ready to "take action" and call. It's based on the real number of at-need deaths combined with the number of consumers willing to preplan. The preplan number can be influenced by marketing. The at-need number, of course, is fixed.

In the next five chapters, we will look at each phase of the Funeral Sales Funnel separately, starting with Awareness – The First

Phase of The Consumer's Journey. The chapter starts with three ways to define funeral homes from a marketing and advertising perspective. And if you'll remember the Reader's Guide at the beginning of the book, I asked you to circle your marketing and advertising style, circle the Funeral Buyer Type you are most interested in, and circle your Funeral Home Type. By doing all three, you are clarifying who you are and what you stand for. That way, when we begin the roadmap, you have a clear and strategic starting point.

A Note from the Author

I find it is necessary to clarify that *The Consumer's Journey to Purchasing Funeral Services* is written from a broad demographic-based perspective allowing you to envision the journey as experienced by most consumers. However, the timing of this journey is unpredictable; for some, it may unfold quickly, while for others, it could span decades. Additionally, it's important to acknowledge the significant diversity among consumers. We are all different. You can't serve everyone, so it's vitally important to focus on the ones you want to do business with you, your "Ideal Consumers." It's why Funeral Buyer Types, as referenced in the Reader's Guide, is pivotal. It details Funeral Buyer Types and sub-types or "personas" in a way that highlights the full range of consumer needs and preferences.

If you believe gaining insights on these Funeral Buyer Types beforehand will benefit your comprehension, then go ahead. Skip to Chapter 8, Funeral Buyer Types. Both Chapter 8 and Chapter 9, Funeral Home Types, will give you a solid foundation that will enhance your understanding of the Journey in subsequent chapters. And if you re-read Chapters 8 and 9 after completing the journey, it will solidify your insights and ensure a more comprehensive understanding.

Key Thoughts from Chapter 2:

1. The "funnel" in marketing and advertising is an accepted, visual metaphor.

2. The funnel can be applied across a broad spectrum of business-to-business and business-to-consumer businesses.

3. A funnel is an ongoing cycle with no definitive endpoint.

4. The Funeral Sales Funnel represents a big-ticket, one-time purchase.

5. There's a finite number of consumers ready to "take action" because it's based on the real number of at-need deaths combined with consumers willing to preplan.

6. The preplan number can be influenced by marketing. The at-need number is fixed.

The Funeral Sales Funnel

Awareness

Interest

Desire

Action

Retention

CHAPTER THREE

Awareness – The First Phase of The Consumer's Journey

If you have decided you are going to bring a change to your business, and change means new marketing and advertising campaigns for the purpose of growing market share, it begins with the consumer during the first phase of The Consumer's Journey. For them to be "aware" of funeral services, and specifically aware of your funeral home, unless you are in a unique or stagnant market, you must be engaged in some form of a marketing and advertising program. As you will read later in the book, "Who Are You Attracting to Your Sales Funnel?" you will want to use The Four Pillars of Effective Local Advertising in Part II to effectively reach your Ideal Consumer for this phase and the next three.

There Are Three Marketing and Advertising Styles for Funeral Homes

I recognize not every funeral home has a formalized marketing and advertising program, so let me help you by defining funeral homes from a marketing and advertising style perspective. It's a part of knowing who you are and what you stand for. That way it will be easier to decide your starting point in the roadmap, and how much of a change you plan to make:

1. **Leader.** Being a Leader means consistently employing innovative marketing and advertising strategies that set a funeral home apart. This includes social media, digital marketing, and mass media using local outlets with a proven, critical mass of Ideal Consumers. A Leader tends to be a visionary, forward-thinker, and actively engaged and involved in the community. A Leader will have a strong reputation built on years of providing exceptional service. The Leader conveys a sense of achievement and distinction that permeates throughout everything they do, including their advertising. They will consistently communicate a high standard of professionalism. Maintaining a Leader status will be foremost on their minds. A Leader will have the biggest audience share of the Funeral Sales Funnel because they have been consistently engaged in advertising and marketing much more so than the other two styles that follow.

2. **Aspirant.** Being an aspirant means there is a strong desire to enhance a funeral home's marketing and advertising strategies but faces challenges in the execution. The Aspirant tends to be eager and an adopter open to change but also more cautious in their approach. The Aspirant

recognizes the importance of social media advertising and digital marketing, yet often finds itself constrained by time, resources, or knowledge. The day-to-day realities, deep commitment to serving families, and limited access to specialized marketing expertise can hinder their progress. Despite these obstacles, Aspirants possess a clear willingness to grow and a latent potential to become a Leader. Aspirants who advertise will have an audience share of consumers in the Funeral Sales Funnel, but not as large as a Leader's.

3. **Essentialist.** Essentialists are focused on the core, indispensable aspects of funeral service. The Essentialist tends to be all about tradition, personal relationships, and the timeless aspects of care and dignity in the grieving process. An Essentialist may be heard saying they do things the same way they have always been done. They may engage in marketing and advertising, but their reluctance to spend money keeps them on the sidelines. Their budgets may be constrained because of limited resources. The Essentialist is heavily reliant on word-of-mouth referrals and the strength of their reputation. To be fair, Essentialists are not resisting change. Instead, they are more committed to tradition and quality of service. The Essentialist will have a minimal share of the Funeral Sales Funnel.

Marketing and Advertising Styles Can Change

I hesitate to broadly label funeral homes as highly competitive, but it's true that competition exists. Growth initiatives, operational changes, responses to new market perceptions, or shifts in the competitive landscape can alter a funeral home's position. For instance, a new owner or newly estab-lished business could immediately adopt a Leader style. Con-versely, the dominant "Premier" funeral home might decide to embrace an Essentialist approach to improve cash flow. This underscores that the status of a firm within a market is not always stagnant.

The First Phase is the Biggest Part of the Funeral Sales Funnel

This first phase at the top of the Funeral Sales Funnel represents the biggest audience or group of consumers you can market to. It's during this phase that a consumer becomes aware of the need for services because they are being exposed to the idea for the first time. Possibly the consumer becomes aware of a brand and a firm through advertising, word of mouth, commu-nity involvement, or simply driving by a funeral home. The key here is that a consumer may recognize a brand, but they haven't started to think about the idea of purchasing funeral services yet. It's not a need, and besides, death happens to others. "It shall happen to thee, but not to me" (Elisabeth Kubler-Ross, 1969).

Reference 1 in the back of the book, The On Phenomenon, describes how a consumer's mind works, and how it has two spheres, the "conscious" and the "subconscious" spheres. What you'll discover is the conscious can only think about one thing at a time. It's incredibly powerful but easily forgets. On the other hand, the subconscious remembers everything like a filing cabi-net. Sigmund Freud, in the book, *The Interpretation of Dreams*, writes, "Nothing can be brought to an end in the unconscious; nothing is past or forgotten" (Freud, 1950).

The Purpose of Advertising in the Awareness and Interest Phases of The Consumer's Journey is to Establish an Equity Position for the Funeral Home in the Minds of its Ideal Consumers.

Leaders will recognize the benefit of advertising during the awareness phase. Whether Leaders know it or not, this is when repetition and consistency establishes trust. And even though a consumer will not actively watch, listen, read, or purposefully remember an ad for a funeral home in the first phase, the subconscious mind retains all experiences and inputs, functioning like a powerful repository of sensations and memories far beyond immediate awareness. It remembers everything. Knowing this, the purpose of advertising in the awareness and interest phases is to establish an equity position for the funeral home in the minds of their Ideal Consumers.

Key Thoughts from Chapter 3:

1. If you intend to grow market share, you must be engaged in some form of advertising during the Awareness Phase.

2. There are three styles of marketing and advertising for funeral homes.

3. "Leader" funeral homes consistently employ innovative marketing and advertising strategies that set a funeral home apart.

4. "Aspirant" funeral homes are open to change, and despite certain obstacles, are willing to grow.

5. "Essentialist" funeral homes are focused on the core aspects of funeral service and heavily reliant on word-of-mouth referrals.

6. The purpose of advertising in the awareness and interest phases is to establish an equity position for a funeral home in the minds of their Ideal Consumers.

The Funeral Sales Funnel

Awareness

Interest

Desire

Action

Retention

CHAPTER

Interest – The Second Phase of The Consumer's Journey

Transitioning from Awareness to Interest can begin when a consumer goes from knowing about a product or service to considering it as an option. Their cognitive state can be characterized by *curiosity*. It's a change that can be the result of something that encourages or initiates a thought, action, or reaction. For example, if a consumer became interested in a newer vehicle, that interest may have started after a series of repairs got them thinking about reliability. Or maybe they traveled somewhere and could have used more space for additional passengers or luggage.

This transition also applies to routine purchases. A consumer may be aware of a new pizza brand or item because of advertising, passing by a store, or hearing about it from friends. The transition from awareness to interest would be much quicker than a big-ticket item, and stem from hunger, convenience, or a craving.

Common factors in the transition from Awareness to Interest is a consumer's growing level of curiosity and passive interest for more information. They may also begin to visualize using a product or service and imagine how it would fit into their life or meet their needs. That could lead to a more personal connection, including beginning to "trust" or have comfort with a brand.

Why Would a Consumer Be Interested in Funeral Homes?

As the Funeral Sales Funnel narrows, so does the number of con-sumers who have transitioned from the Awareness phase to the Interest phase. It's a somewhat smaller audience than the Aware-ness audience. Why would a consumer suddenly be interested in funeral homes? What may have encouraged or initiated a thought, action, or reaction? It might have been sparked by something as simple as celebrating a 60th birthday, when loved ones exchange over-the-hill cards, and cakes and gifts are adorned in black, humorously symbolizing mortality. As a consumer gets older, age milestones can prompt introspection and consideration of one's legacy, and thus, create interest.

Another reason could be something is happening with a friend or someone they know. Maybe they went to a visitation or cel-ebration of life at a funeral home. Before or after it, they read an obituary on Facebook or the funeral home's website. And since interested consumers are curious, they could have spent time reading other obituaries, looking for other people that they knew, and explored other parts of the funeral home's website. Taking it a step further, this is a time when they might research a firm's reviews. Reading reviews by customers can offer insights into real experiences from people like them and help shape their decision-making process as they enter Phase 3 – Desire.

"The Purpose of Advertising in the Awareness and Interest Phases of The Consumer's Journey is to Establish an Equity Position for the Funeral Home in the Minds of its Ideal Consumers."

A consumer in the Interest phase does not believe they will need funeral services anytime soon, so just like in the Awareness phase, they will probably not actively watch, listen, read, or purposefully remember an ad for a funeral home. If you are a Leader funeral home, and you're advertising, you're establishing an equity position in your Ideal Consumer's mind. Some call it nurturing. A later chapter called "Educating the Consumer" will give you insights on what topics an interested consumer would be attracted to.

The next chapter, Desire – The Third Phase of The Consumer's Journey, is one of the most important chapters in the book. It describes a consumer triggered by a significant event. Funeral homes actively advertising in Phases 1 and 2 will suddenly and perceptually be heard and trusted. That's because consumers in the Desire phase will actively watch, listen, read, or purposefully remember their advertising.

If there is no Leader or Aspirant in the market, consumers may enter the Desire phase without strong preconceived notions or preferences shaped by brand advertising or education. This could mean the consumer's desires and decision-making process is more influenced by immediate needs, personal referrals, word of mouth, or basic services found on a Google search.

Key Thoughts from Chapter 4:

1. Transitioning from Awareness to Interest can begin when a consumer goes from knowing about a product or service to considering it as an option.

2. Common factors in the transition from Awareness to Interest is a consumer's growing level of *curiosity* and passive interest for more information.

3. As a consumer gets older, age milestones can prompt introspection and consideration of one's legacy, and thus, create interest.

4. Another reason for interest could be something is happening with a friend or someone they know.

5. The purpose of advertising in the Awareness and Interest phases of The Consumer's Journey is to establish an equity position for the funeral home in the minds of its Ideal Consumers.

The Funeral Sales Funnel

Awareness

Interest

Desire

Action

Retention

CHAPTER FIVE

Desire – The Third Phase of The Consumer's Journey

When a consumer enters the Desire phase of a sales funnel, they evolve from a general interest in a product or service to developing a specific desire for it. For example, someone with a growing family looking for a home might transition from wanting a bigger space to specifically looking for a home in a certain neighborhood because of its schools, community, average size, and resale value.

On the other end of the spectrum, for everyday purchases, a consumer's interest in food may quickly turn into desire when they are hungry and it is time to eat. Here the consumer is making a decision about satisfying an immediate want or need rather than a long-term investment.

In both examples, the emotional connection to a product or service begins to solidify, making it a critical point in the sales funnel when advertisers reinforce their brand or differentiate themselves from other providers.

A Consumer Enters The Desire Phase When They Have Been Triggered.

A consumer enters the Desire phase of The Funeral Sales Funnel when they've been triggered by a significant event or shocking information that makes the need for funeral services more immediate. The news could be the consumer has received a terminal diagnosis, or a close family member's serious health issue has taken a turn. In either case, "death" is suddenly foremost on their mind.

It's a problem. The biggest problem they will ever face. And unlike the homes, cars, and food scenarios, where the consumer is transitioning from Interest to Desire based on positive aspirations or a "want," in funeral services it is based on a "need," a need that is at the core of their new emotions including resistance and resentment.

"Death is never possible in regard to ourselves." - Elisabeth Kubler-Ross, M.D.

When the consumer has the need, they must reach the emotion of acceptance. That's not an easy or immediate process. Elisabeth Kubler-Ross, M.D., in her book, *On Death & Dying*, writes, "When we look back in time and study old cultures and people, we are impressed that death has always been distasteful to man and will probably always be. From a psychiatrist's point of view this is very understandable and can perhaps best be explained by our basic knowledge that, in our unconscious, death is never possible in regard to ourselves. It is inconceivable for our unconscious to imagine an actual ending of our own life here on earth" (Elisabeth Kubler-Ross, 1969). Translated: the consumer's first emotions include denial.

Dr. Kubler-Ross goes on to say, "Emotional life is complex, ... sometimes seemingly incompatible states, such as denial and acceptance, can coexist." But whether it's denial or acceptance, death will easily dominate their conscious thinking. It will be one of their first thoughts when waking to begin a new day, and most likely it will be the last thought on their mind when they finally fall asleep. It's during these times, just waking or falling asleep, they are in a state of relaxed awareness and reduced critical thinking. *These are the moments thoughts and ideas are more easily imprinted on their subconscious mind.* Combined with thoughts throughout the day as they are living their life, repeated conscious consideration can shape deeper perceptions and feelings in a way that future behaviors and preferences are shaped.

Sigmond Freud describes it like this: "I believe that the conscious wish becomes effective in exciting a dream only when it succeeds in arousing a similar unconscious 'wish' which reinforces it" (Freud, 1950). You remember Aladdin? "Your wish is my command."

"Your subconscious mind is dedicated to bringing into your life what you're thinking about most of the time."

Leading figures in the field of personal development and self-help who are experts on the power of the subconscious mind, and how it is dedicated to bringing into your life what you think about most of the time, are relevant here. Napoleon Hill (*Think and Grow Rich*, 1937) and Rhonda Byrne (*The Secret*, 2006) say it like this: "Thoughts become things." Cast members in Byrne's movie constantly repeat the phrase, "Your wish is my command." Translated: your subconscious mind is dedicated to bringing into your life what you're thinking about most of the time.

"Marketing is the generous act of helping someone solve a problem. Their problem." - Seth Godin

---

Clearly the consumer is facing the ultimate challenge of their lifetime. It's a problem and it needs to be solved. Seth Godin, in his book, *This is Marketing: You Can't Be Seen Until You Learn to See*, writes, "Marketing is the generous act of helping someone solve a problem. *Their problem*" (Godin, 2018). As a funeral home, that's the way to look at your marketing effort. Helping a prospective customer solve a problem.

Acceptance

When the consumer achieves the emotion of acceptance, they may begin to explore specific details and options. What kind of funeral do they want? Will it be cremation or a traditional service? If it's traditional, where will they be buried? Who will be there? Will their friends be there? Will it be religious? Does it have to be? And ultimately, what you're most interested in if you're reading this book, *where will it be? Who can do this for me?* Many questions will be asked and answered, and over time the consumer may ask family and friends for advice as they shape what they would like to see for themselves or maybe a loved one. They can also be influenced by marketing and advertising.

This is the time when the consumer's subconscious mind is trying to solve the problem, fulfill their wish, attract answers, and ultimately bring the needed funeral services into their life. From a marketing and advertising perspective, it's the time they become fully "aware" or "On" for buying funeral services (The "On Phenomenon," Reference 1). Funeral Home advertising now seemingly appears out of nowhere with a certain amount of predictability and frequency. That's the subconscious mind in action. This is when ads that were consistently running in the Awareness and Interest phases and forgotten in the past (but stored in their subconscious) are now being consciously watched, listened to, read, and purposefully <u>remembered</u>.

The Preplanner

In Chapter 8, Funeral Buyer Types, you'll discover there are multiple personas for The Preplanner. What makes The Preplanner different is the trigger that transitions them to Phase 3 – Desire is not based on immediacy. Death is not expected in the next 30-60 days. Triggers can span from aging, a health diagnosis, or experiencing a close loss, to their desire for controlling the next phase in their life and the lives of their loved ones. Their steps to taking action as described in the next chapter will be the same as any other consumer. It's just the sense of urgency is far less.

The next chapter, Action – The Fourth Phase of The Consumer's Journey, is when decisions are formulated, and calls are made. Will your firm be the only and obvious choice?

Key Thoughts from Chapter 5:

1. The Desire phase of the sales funnel can best be described as when the emotional connection to a product or service begins to solidify.

2. A consumer enters the Desire phase of The Funeral Sales Funnel when they are triggered by a significant event or shocking information, and funeral services are more immediate.

3. Funeral services are based on a "need."

4. Marketing is the generous act of helping someone solve a problem. *Their* problem. – Seth Godin

5. When the consumer achieves the emotion of acceptance, they may begin to explore specific details and options.

6. Consumers in the Desire phase are "On" for buying funeral services.

7. Advertising by funeral homes in the Desire phase seemingly appears out of nowhere with a certain amount of predictability and frequency.

The Funeral Sales Funnel

Awareness

Interest

Desire

Action

Retention

CHAPTER SIX

Action – The Fourth Phase of The Consumer's Journey

This is it, the smallest phase of the sales funnel. The Action phase is when a decision is made and a purchase is completed. Example, for everyday purchases, a consumer decides what they want, drives and buys, or has delivered. Unlike a purchase of a lifetime like a home, the funnel can start as early as later in the day or the day after.

Big-ticket items, like vehicles, will have consumers engaged in detailed research like comparing models, pricing, features, and financing. They may go to one or more dealerships, take test drives, and when they have their financing in place, during one of those trips, a salesperson is going to ask the right questions and get the deal done.

Funerals are not as big of an item as a car or a house, but perceptually still expensive, making this a big-ticket funnel, meaning it may only happen a few times in someone's life. What makes it unique is the added emotional complexity due to the nature of the service.

Initial Decision Making

If death is imminent or has just occurred, the consumer is in an emotional state. And unlike other big-ticket items where you have time to be thoughtful, the need for funeral services comes with an inherent urgency. Decisions must be made in a relatively short timeframe.

If the decision wasn't made during the Desire phase, the consumer would consider what kind of service they want, from traditional to cremation to alternative. They may be considering services, too, like a visitation or celebration of life. Conversely, their thoughts may be grounded in cost, leading them to a process of making price comparisons.

"When a consumer reaches the Action phase, they either know who they trust and know who they are calling, or they don't."

In the book *Positioning: The Battle for your Mind* (Reis and Trout, 2001), the authors describe the concept of a mental ladder, where brand preferences are ranked on a product ladder in their mind. But according to Alan Creedy, a funeral industry expert

(Two Guys and a Question), his conversation with these authors revealed that, in the funeral industry, consumers are different in that they tend to have only one brand on their product ladder or "consideration set."

If that's your funeral home, if you are the one brand they trust the most, and you've created a clear, compelling, and easy call-to-action in your advertising, it may motivate them to take the final step with you. The goal is to be the only and obvious choice or at least the first or preferred choice. In a perfect world, they are using Google as the white pages and searching for you and your firm. In this case you may not feel the need to be invested in SEO and Google AdWords.

If you are not advertising during the Awareness and Interest phases, and if no other funeral home has established an equity position in the consumer's mind, then action may start with their searching the web with phrases like "funeral homes near me," "cremation services," or "pre-planning funeral services." That's when investing in SEO and Google AdWords can be practical and logical. Consider this though: your firm is now on a list along with other firms you compete with. How does a consumer differentiate you versus them? If you're using the right keywords, the ad copy is compelling, and you are fully optimized for website search engines, you can generate activity.

> *"Will your funeral home be the only and obvious choice?"*

The final choice of a funeral service provider is influenced by numerous factors, cost, perceived value, the funeral home's reputation, personal recommendations, convenience, location, tradition, and much more. Simply put, there are <u>many</u> considerations. This leads to an important question: will your funeral home emerge as the only and obvious choice? I believe it's why you're reading this book. If you're formulating what change looks like to expand your market share and revenue, you need to have a firm grasp on knowing who you are and what you stand for. With that thought foremost in your mind, consider the following three questions. They are designed to help you identify a starting point on your roadmap to growth:

Question 1: What kind of advertising or marketing strategy do you plan to use?

As we step into Part II of this book, we will expand on these two types of advertising or marketing strategies to choose from. You can be engaged in one or both. They are:

- **Brand Advertising** that builds brand awareness and establishes an image or perception. It is a long-term strategy with bigger growth potential that takes time to build. Leaders tend to be engaged in Brand Advertising throughout the entire consumer's journey.

- **Direct Marketing** elicits a direct response from a target market that is about to make a purchase. It is a short-term strategy that's focused on immediate results. Direct Marketing advertises to older audiences more likely to need services because of their age, stage in life, and where they live.

Question 2: How would you define your style as it relates to your marketing and advertising?

If you'll recall, Chapter 3 defines a funeral home's marketing and advertising style. Circle yours. To review:

- **Leader** consistently employs innovative marketing and advertising.
- **Aspirant** has a strong desire but is more cautious and somewhat limited.
- **Essentialist** is heavily reliant on word of mouth and referrals.

Question 3: What is your Funeral Home Type?

Here are three that are relevant to this chapter:

- **Premier** is the funeral home that leads in market share and perceptually is the most trusted.
- **Emerging** is new, under new leadership, or recently purchased.
- **Plateaued** defines a funeral home that appears to be stable but slowly losing market share.

Where Do You Start?

If you're a Premier funeral home with a marketing and advertising style of Leader, then the effort to "change" could be very small. Your answer to grow revenue may come to you after reading Chapter 12, How to Grow a Business. Most likely, a Premier funeral home that's a Leader is doing both Brand Advertising and Direct Marketing while maintaining or protecting their Leader style.

If you're an Emerging funeral home and your advertising style is Aspirant, then your effort to "change" may not be so nuanced. You may decide to want to be a Premier funeral home, and thus, the marketing and advertising style needs to be transformed from Aspirant to Leader.

For Plateaued funeral homes, there are lots of opportunities.

The next chapter is the final phase of The Consumer's Journey, Retention. It's the most obvious place to apply organic marketing for long-term success.

Key Thoughts from Chapter 6:

1. The Action Phase is when a decision is made and a purchase is completed.

2. Funeral industry consumers are different in that they tend to have only one brand on their product ladder or "consideration set."

3. Unlike other big-ticket items, the need for funeral services comes with an inherent urgency.

4. When a consumer reaches the Action phase, they either know who they trust and they know who they're calling, or they don't.

5. Answering the three questions will help you formulate a starting point on the roadmap in Part II.

The Funeral Sales Funnel

Awareness

Interest

Desire

Action

Retention

CHAPTER SEVEN

Retention – The Fifth Phase of The Consumer's Journey.

There are two audiences in the Retention phase, the first being those who have purchased a preplanned funeral. For consumers who have purchased a preplanned funeral, communication through email or newsletters updating them on new services or community involvement can reinforce their choice. Depending on their age, you may offer annual reviews of their plan to make any adjustment as a result of a life change. You might also consider a partnership with a trusted attorney or financial planner who can offer quarterly events or seminars on estate planning. Whatever you do, it is vitally important they feel cared for beyond the contract they signed. Birthday cards, holiday greetings, or any personal touches will strengthen your relationship.

The second audience is much bigger: surviving family members and families you have served. These are consumers who know you intimately, and you know them. They have witnessed your professionalism, have been guided by your expertise, and experienced some of the most difficult times in their lives alongside you or a member of your firm. It's a close, personal relationship unlike any other.

It's vitally important to maintain relationships through compassionate aftercare services. Grief support, whether in a group setting or using a third party sending personalized messages honoring the anniversary of a death, nurtures them and keeps them connected.

"What consumers say about you carries genuine authenticity and truth."

Physically bringing families together is another powerful strategy. Community events like an Easter Sunrise Service, a 4th of July parade, a picnic and live music for Veterans on Veteran's Day, or a Christmas Candlelight Service are the kinds of events where people come together. Not only do they get to see you again, but they can also interact with other families who share their stories about their experiences with your funeral home. What consumers say about you carries genuine authenticity and truth.

With both audiences, ongoing advertising campaigns can play a huge role in retention. Staying top-of-mind with past clients, reinforcing their positive experiences, and maintaining a connection can offer comfort even when it's not directly related to an imme-diate need. For a consumer in the retention phase, encountering the funeral director who served them – whether through a Face-book post or a radio/TV ad – can have a profound impact. They are the kind of reminders that vividly reinforce their previous experience and solidify the perception that your funeral home is the only and obvious choice for future needs.

Grief support as a topic is retention.

Grief support is a common, traditional topic especially used by funeral homes on social media. Its role in marketing and adver-tising is retention. It makes sense as an ongoing campaign. Just be sure it's not the only campaign you are running. That's because it does not speak to or reach consumers in Phases 1, 2, and 3.

In the next chapter, I am going to describe Funeral Buyer Types. Matching buyer types to the audiences you are targeting will make it easier to craft the right messaging. If marketing means changing the way consumers think about funeral services, then realize, "you have no chance of changing everyone" (Godin, 2018).

Key Thoughts from Chapter 7:

1. There are two audiences in the Retention phase, those who have preplanned and surviving family members and families you have served.

2. Have a plan to communicate with those who have pur-chased a preplanned funeral.

3. It's vitally important to maintain relationships with surviving family members through compassionate aftercare services.

4. Physically bringing families together is a powerful strategy.

5. What consumers say about you carries genuine authenticity and truth.

CHAPTER EIGHT

Funeral Buyer Types

Funeral buyer types are diverse categories of consumers or "thinking patterns" based on their behavior, motivations, and needs when purchasing funeral services. As a result of my research, buyer types can vary widely from funeral home to funeral home. And even though a funeral home can have more than one buyer type, practically all a funeral home's customers will have something in common: where they live or lived.

> *"Funeral homes are community-centered businesses catering to the needs of families in neighborhoods and localities."*

Funeral homes are community-centered businesses catering to the needs of families in neighborhoods and localities. This local aspect is key when thinking about geography, as well as the demographic and psychographic realities of the people who live in a funeral home's area of service. For firms with two or three locations, it would not be uncommon for them to have very different buyer types at each location. It would also be fair to say that these realities can evolve over time as people move in and out of an area due to employment, opportunities, neighborhood improvements or degradations, and other market conditions you have no control over.

The goal of this chapter is to help you see there are many different buyer types and personas, and how important it is to have the one or ones you are trying to persuade, inform, and remind at the forefront of your mind. Knowing them and naming them will give you some clarity as you approach planning your marketing, your advertising, your media, and your messaging strategies to achieve better revenue outcomes.

There are four primary Funeral Buyer Types, and within each exist distinct "buyer personas" or "thinking patterns" that embody specific preferences, needs, and behaviors. As we'll discuss in Chapter 18, they can also be defined as "thinking patterns." The four buyer types are:

1. **The Immediate, "At-Need" Buyer**. These are buyers prepared to purchase funeral services immediately because death is imminent or someone has died. They prioritize their needs quickly and are driven to make fast decisions. Immediate buyers have the greatest number of personas including:

    a. The loyal buyer (can also be called a follower): Their family has always used your funeral home. There is no question they are going to call you. No other firm has been successful with marketing to change their decision. You are the one.

b. The second timer (can also be a loyal buyer): This is someone who bought a funeral one time, experienced the process, and the second (or third) time around will better know what they want or don't want.

c. The caring buyer (can also be the ultimate buyer): They deeply care about the deceased, and simply want the best. Price is not as important as the way they feel. If it costs more or costs the most, that's okay and the right thing to do. A statement is made, unquestionable compassion is communicated.

d. The whole family buyer: Everyone has to be there. The process takes longer to explain because everyone comprehends differently. Bathroom and cigarette breaks disrupt the flow. When the whole family is not present, another meeting may take place before final decisions are made. When the whole buyer family becomes complicated, it can lead to…

e. The dysfunctional family buyer: Everyone doesn't get along, everyone may not be there because they don't like each other, and they test everyone's limits, especially yours.

f. The disconnected buyer (can also be the disposer – an unattractive word that many I interviewed insisted we use): The disconnected buyer has other things to do in their life, so their decision-making process is based on convenience, their calendar, and not conflicting with their schedule and personal commitments.

g. The shocked buyer: They had no idea this was going to happen, they simply didn't know what to do, so they showed up at your funeral home. When they heard the pricing, they were shocked by the cost. They run to their car, go away, maybe they come back. This buyer can also be described as the uninformed buyer.

h. New to town buyer: They are new to the area and got word-of-mouth advertising from new friends.

i. The influenced buyer: This is a buyer who was influenced to call you based on something you or someone else has been doing for them. They could have been on the receiving end of a kind act. When they visited your funeral home to deliver something like the mail or flowers, you had clean restrooms and fresh bananas or a bottle of water. They may have attended a visitation or service and made a connection based on the whole experience.

j. The faith or cultural buyer: This persona goes across multiple buyer types. They come to your funeral home because you are known for providing community-specific needs based on faith, ethnicity, traditions, or culture.

k. The non-religious or "none" buyer: This is another persona that spans across multiple buyer types. According to Pew Research (Smith, December 14, 2021), about three in ten adults define themselves as non-religious which includes atheists, agnostics, or those who described themselves as not affiliated with any organized religion.

2. **The Preplanner.** This is the top buyer type that can be influenced by marketing as evidenced by the prevalence

of marketing firms in the industry. Preplanners are buying for themselves or a loved one in advance. Personas can include:

a. The planner buyer: This is someone who, over their lifetime, has done an outstanding job of planning for the family. They planned to have a family, planned for college expenses, planned their financial future with a financial planner, and now they are going to plan a funeral.

b. The financial planner: This is someone who is driven to preplan because they are practical. The financial planner is motivated by cost savings and financial benefits. The concept of "locking in" a price to secure today's pricing for future services is attractive to them.

c. The inspired planner: This is a person who recently experienced a funeral, either for someone in their family or someone close to them. Their experience was compelling enough that they thought to themselves that this should be taken care of in advance, so that this time it would be easier for everyone.

d. The courageous planner: This buyer wants to take the first step but is hesitant. Maybe they have done a lot of reading or investigating but have not really shared their feelings with others. It's a private personal experience that may go so far as driving to the funeral home, sitting in the parking lot, and then, after thinking it through, driving away. But at some point, they are going to call or walk in because they have built themselves up to the point where they have achieved the courage to move forward. When they finally do it, they are relieved and wonder why they struggled.

e. The transferred preplanner: This is someone who either bought a planned funeral and moved to your area, or they live in your area and, for whatever reason, decided to transfer their plan. It could be they were following a funeral director from one firm to the next, heard something that was disconcerting, or made a new connection that put the idea in their mind.

f. The authoritative planner (also the decisive planner): They are confident, assertive, and make decisions they feel are best for the family based on their perceptions of what the ideal arrangements should be. The surviving family members may not agree, but it's how they've always rolled.

g. The storyteller (also a persona for buyer type 4, the customizer): They want to use the funeral experience to tell a life story using multimedia, as well as having friends and family sharing specific stories and milestones. This cannot be done in a few days, which is why it would make sense for the storyteller to preplan.

"When price is the issue, it's the only issue."

---

3. **The Price Sensitive Buyer.** What I always say when asked about these kinds of buyers, "When price is the issue, it's the only issue." Price sensitive buyers are, without a doubt, the fastest growing buyer type. More and more, the phone rings and it's a consumer asking about pricing. Their focus is primarily on cost and affordability. Buyer personas include:

a. The investigator: This is a big-ticket item to them. Just like the car buyer who researches trade-in values and vehicle prices, they are using the internet/search engines as tools to figure out if you are the right funeral home to use, but most importantly, at the right price.

b. The shopper: This individual will be a little more casual in their approach versus the investigator who will be more thorough. The shopper is doing exactly that, shopping around without any real strategy. They will ask about prices because they think they're supposed to, but they also want to know about the process.

c. The lowest price buyer: They don't care who you are, how long you have been in business, or even your reputation. They want the lowest or cheapest. Period.

d. The broke buyer: This is also a growing category. They may care, they may be sad, they may be pathetic, they may have a compelling story, and they have no money!

e. The minimalist (eco-friendly could also fit here): These buyers are motivated by their concern for the earth. They are overtly interested in simplicity and sustainability, but whether they are willing to admit it or not, price is also a consideration which is why it fits in this buyer type.

f. The disconnected buyer described in the immediate need buyer type also fits here.

4. **The Customizer**. This buyer type is most interested in personalizing services that reflect the unique life of the deceased. A customizer can also be a preplanner. A customizer will love working with a certified celebrant. Personas can include:

a. The faith or cultural buyer: They have unique needs and want to be sure the funeral adheres to their traditions and defined religion's rules.

b. The celebrator: This is a persona that gets it. The celebrator will go beyond the norms. Where the funeral is held, when it's held, who says what, the live music, the party, the fun! The deceased wanted to go out this way and not put their friends in an uncomfortable situation.

c. The authoritative buyer: As described in preplanning, they have all the answers. Their preconceived ideas and strong convictions may not be the norm, but they know best.

d. The minimalist (also a Price Sensitive buyer): This buyer is making an understatement in the service, focusing on the essence versus the scale of the event.

e. Eco-Conscious Buyer: This is all about the green experience. What's the smallest footprint? How do we honor the earth? What's the minimal environmental impact?

f. The storyteller is a persona that wants to use the funeral experience to tell the life story of the deceased. The storyteller is also a preplanner because the story takes time to create. They will use multimedia, as well as have friends and family share specific stories and milestones.

As you read through these buyer types and personas, let me say I am sure there are other personas that I have missed. I'd love to hear yours. And although this may not be the most comprehensive list in the industry, it should be broad enough and deep enough to be a benefit to you as you market to your Ideal Consumer on their journey.

"You can't serve everyone."

You can't serve everyone. Knowing the four buyer types and their associated personas can begin to provide you with some clarity that will make it easier to tailor a marketing approach to meet the specific needs and preferences of your ideal customer. It also sets the stage for us to help you build the marketing roadmap for growing market share and revenue.

The next chapter looks at Funeral Home Types. By knowing your Funeral Home Type and associating your advertising style, it's easier to define who you are and what you stand for when you begin to create your roadmap.

Key Thoughts from Chapter 8:

1. Even though a funeral home can have multiple buyer types, most of its customers will have something in common: where they live or lived.

2. Knowing Funeral Buyer Types or "thinking patterns" will give you clarity as you plan your marketing, advertising, media, and messaging strategies.

3. There are four Funeral Buyer Types: immediate "At-Need" buyers, The Preplanners, Price Sensitive buyers, and buyers who want their experience customized.

4. Buyer type personas embody specific preferences, needs, and behaviors.

5. You can't serve everyone. Knowing funeral home buyer types is a first step to better defining the consumers you want to attract to your funeral home.

Funeral Home Types

Exploring Funeral Buyer Types through conversations with customers was truly enlightening. Each had a unique perspective influenced by who they are, what they stand for, market conditions, and where they are located. While the list of Funeral Buyer Types I've compiled may not be the most exhaustive in the industry, it is both broad and detailed enough to serve our needs. It's leading you up to a later chapter when I introduce the concept of matching consumer thinking patterns (encompassing Funeral Buyer Types and their personas) with different Funeral Home Types, which is the focus for this chapter.

Again, this list of Funeral Home Types may not be the industry's most comprehensive list but having the benefit of talking to and physically visiting hundreds of funeral homes, it should cover most. They are:

- **"The Premier Funeral Home."** This is a funeral home that leads in market share, and perceptually is the most trusted. Depending on market size, there can be more than one. Characteristics can include:
  - Community focused. This firm actively engages in and supports local community activities.
  - Family-Owned. This firm emphasizes its history, tradition, personal touch, and compassionate care.
  - Corporately owned firms benefit from professional management expertise, access to capital to build and maintain high-quality facilities, and innovative practices to enhance customer experience.

- **"The Emerging Funeral Home."** This is a funeral home that is new to the market, an established firm with new leadership, or an established firm that has been recently purchased. Characteristics can include:
  - Community focused. Similar to the Premier Funeral Home, the Emerging Funeral Home may choose this strategy.
  - A rising star in a corporate environment is given a new opportunity to turn a situation around. It's a fresh face driven by new leadership with a vision.
  - Family-Owned. Emphasis on "our family serving yours" and compassionate care.

- **"The Plateaued Funeral Home."** This defines a funeral home operating at a level where noticeable growth has stalled. It may seem stable, but slow erosion of market share may be occurring due to unchanged practices, lack of resources, or tired leadership.

- **"The Innovator Funeral Home."** This is a funeral home that incorporates modern, possibly non-traditional services. It's forward thinking, adaptable, and capable of meeting diverse needs and preferences. A Premier or Emerging Funeral Home can be an Innovator, but an Innovator Funeral Home can also stand on its own. It may have a focus using Certified Celebrants. It could also have a banquet facility for parties and receptions. Green could fit here, too.

- **"The Price Strategy Funeral Home."** This funeral home is attractive to consumers who are motivated by a low price. Some may use price as a strategy to get prospective customers through the door, and then apply sales tactics to grow the final price. Direct cremation services would be based on Price Strategy.

- **"The Specialty Funeral Home."** This is a funeral home that focuses on a specific religious, ethnic, or cultural service. A Specialty Funeral Home can also be known as a Premier Funeral Home in the community they serve.

How to Look at Funeral Home Types with a Marketing and Advertising Style

Being the Premier funeral home in a market doesn't always mean it has the style of a Leader. On the contrary, the Premier funeral home could easily have an Essentialist style. It may be in a market that is geographically closed, and they are clearly the only funeral home servicing an area. It could also be all the firms in the community, regardless of their Funeral Home Type, are Plateaued.

Another way to look at it is there can be more than one Premier funeral home, or possibly a market with no Premier funeral home but rather two Emerging funeral homes with different styles. One could be an Essentialist, while the other is an Aspirant on its way to being a Leader. Are you growing or shrinking?

And there's nothing wrong with being an Essentialist. If your market conditions support it and your business model is profitable, your strategy to grow revenue may be found in Chapter 12, How do you Grow a Business? and considering changing sales processes and enhancing services with existing customers.

Key Thoughts from Chapter 9:

1. The Premier funeral home leads in market share and is perceptually the most trusted.

2. The Emerging funeral home is new, under new leadership, or recently purchased.

3. The Innovator incorporates modern, possibly non-traditional services. Its focus can include a certified celebrant.

4. The Price Strategy funeral home attracts consumers where price is the issue and it's the only issue.

5. A Specialty funeral home focus can be religious, ethnic, or cultural.

6. A Plateaued funeral home is either stagnant or losing market share.

7. Associating Funeral Home Types with Marketing and Advertising Styles can be instructional when deciding how much change you need to make to grow market share and revenue.

CHAPTER TEN

What Makes Funeral Homes Unique?

You may not see this, but first-time visitors and new consumers do. They feel it, too. Walking into a funeral home for the first time and seeing a dead person provokes a profound first impression that's hard to forget. It's not like visiting a car dealer or a furniture store where you're eagerly approached by an anxious salesperson. No. A funeral home is quiet. Eerily quiet. It envelopes them as soon as the door behind them is closed shut. And when they're warmly greeted by a staff member, outwardly they may receive a friendly smile and hearty handshake, but deep inside they know this same person can guide them down a hall or around a corner to encounter an experience they may not feel entirely ready to face.

"Death is never possible in regard to ourselves." – Elisabeth Kubler-Ross

In her book, *On Death & Dying*, Elisabeth Kubler-Ross, M.D. writes "...death is never possible in regard to ourselves" (Elisabeth Kubler-Ross, 1969). Maybe that's why some people are apprehensive about going to a funeral home. A funeral home is a place where there can be conflict between their subconscious belief of immortality and the reality of mortality. It's called cognitive dissonance, defined as a clash between held beliefs and the realities they face. The result is feelings of discomfort or tension.

> ## *"The oldest and strongest kind of fear is fear of the unknown."*
> ### *– H.P. Lovecraft*

Another factor for first-time visitors or consumers is fear of the unknown. H.P. Lovecraft, author of the book, *Supernatural Horror in Literature*, confers, "The oldest and strongest emotion of mankind is fear, and the oldest and strongest kind of fear is fear of the unknown." For the public, you must admit there are a lot of unknowns about what you do and what happens behind the walls where you work.

There's also an aura surrounding a funeral home that carries a profound sense of mystery. It's a physical place where countless souls have come and gone for the last time. And it's not a church but it feels like one. Regardless of their faith, as they contemplate the tangible meeting of the eternal, they may be finding themselves introspectively questioning their beliefs. That's because a funeral home is a place of transition where the connection between life and the physical and the intangible and the eternal are seen and felt.

As you visualize the Consumer's Journey entering Phase 3 – Desire, the truth is a funeral service is not something they desire or want. They want a new car, they want beautiful furniture, and they want to enjoy delicious food. But do they want their teeth drilled into by the dentist or want to file their taxes? No. They don't want to, but they *need* to. You know this. Funeral services are not something a consumer wants but they're something a consumer *needs*.

"Funeral Homes Create Tension."

What makes a funeral home unique? From a marketing and advertising perspective, especially for first-time visitors or consumers, just the thought of a funeral home creates *tension*. Defined, tension is an emotional or cognitive feeling a consumer gets when their needs or desires clash with their current realities or perceptions.

What's the good news? Funeral homes create *tension*. Let me explain why that's a good thing. Seth Godin states, "Marketers who cause change cause tension" (Godin, 2018). There's no doubt, funeral homes that engage in marketing and advertising are positioning themselves to help the consumer *change* the way they think about funeral services. He goes on to say that tension is not the same as fear, yet we have vividly described in this chapter the consumer's initial fear. But Godin remarks, "There might be fear, but tension is the promise that we can get through that fear to the other side." Well put!

"Your Mission is to Establish Trust by Educating and Informing the Consumer."

How does a funeral home successfully relieve tension? According to Godin, "forward motion relieves that tension." To me, that implies how in Phase 2 – Interest, older, curious consumers will begin to explore the possibilities and learn more. And if there is one single idea you get from reading this book, it is simply this: Before the consumer enters Phase 3 – Desire, *"Your mission is to establish trust by educating and informing the consumer."* Not *selling* the consumer but educating and informing the consumer. Based on your style, the *selling* part comes in the arrangement room.

And that's what one of the final chapters in the book is about, how forward motion can begin by educating the consumer. You see, you're in a business that most consumers have little prior knowledge of or experience with until the need arises (Phase 3 – Desire). *Education and information can significantly contribute to creating trust.* By providing clear, helpful, trust-building education and information using The Informative Advertising Style with real people during Phases 1 and 2 of the Consumer's Journey, they may feel more confident and secure when they enter Phase 4 and decide your funeral home is the only and obvious choice.

Key Thoughts from Chapter 10:

1. A funeral home is a place where there can be conflict between the consumer's subconscious belief of immortality and the reality of mortality.

2. Fear is a factor. "The oldest and strongest kind of fear is fear of the unknown."

3. Funeral service is not something the consumer wants. It's something they *need*.

4. A funeral home is not a church but it feels like one.

5. What makes a funeral home unique? Funeral homes create tension.

6. Forward motion relieves tension.

7. Your mission is to establish trust by educating and informing the consumer.

If I Can Be of Assistance To You

Thank you for reading my book. Part I should give you plenty to think about. If after reading Part II you decide you need some help, please feel free to call me. My phone number is 336-516-9163. You can also visit my website, https://PostandBoost.com. There you will find out more about our company, and you can use the convenient links to set up an appointment.

PART II

Developing Your Marketing Roadmap for Growing Market Share and Revenue

CHAPTER ELEVEN

The Difference Between Marketing and Advertising

The roadmap begins! And with any map, you need a place to start and a place to finish. Of course, a key thought with marketing and advertising for any firm is that the marketing never stops. That's because the Funeral Sales Funnel never stops.

Do you know who you are? Do you know what you stand for? And where will you be starting from? Are you a Leader funeral home that has an active marketing plan? Do you buy advertising? Are you investing 5-10% of revenue back into marketing and advertising? Or are you an Aspirant funeral home operator with good intentions, but you're time starved? You know it's vitally important to have a plan to grow, but if you're not fully staffed, you're always working, and families come first, this is a task that's perpetually put off to another day, or next month, or maybe even next year.

But here's a forecast. I'm predicting you would find the time to build and execute a marketing plan to grow market share if it all wasn't so confusing. And right off the top, what's the difference between "marketing" and "advertising"? Isn't *that* confusing? Yes. It is. And when there's confusion, it can lead to indecision, inefficiency, and missed opportunities. Reducing confusion is crucial for strategic progress, so let's start.

"Marketing" and "Advertising" are mistakenly used interchangeably.

The words "marketing" and "advertising" are often used interchangeably but they encompass distinct aspects of promoting any business or service. Marketing is a broader strategy that includes market research, product or service design, audience targeting (your Ideal Consumer), and brand building. With marketing, you should have a clear understanding of your Ideal Consumer's needs and create value that meets those needs. It also includes designing your message and determining how, when, and to whom it should be delivered.

Advertising is a component of marketing. It's the promotion of products and services using the media that can target audiences that reach your Ideal Consumers. For years, advertising would have been defined as mass media consisting of television, radio, newspaper, and billboards. Today, it can include these mass media, but it should always include Meta Platforms (Facebook and Instagram).

Is Marketing More Than You Think?

If you know who you are and you know what you stand for, and you know your Funeral Home Type and the Funeral Buyer Types you wish to attract to your firm, then all of that should be reflected in your marketing. For example, as you think about consumers you are converting to customers, when they visit your funeral home, what will that experience be like? From parking their car and entering your doors, to who greets them, what they say, where they wait, what the arrangement room looks like, what's in it, and the services and merchandise you offer, all of that is marketing.

Since the purpose of this chapter is defining the difference between marketing and advertising, here is a small list of marketing topics and tasks:

- Market Research: Defining your geography, identifying your ideal customer(s), and knowing what their needs are.

- Developing Products and Services: This is tailoring your services to meet the needs of your Ideal Consumers.

- Branding: What is your brand? Does it quickly and clearly establish your Funeral Home Type, or the Funeral Home Type you want to be?

- Digital Marketing: Your website, online reviews, and Facebook/Instagram pages.

- Community Engagement: Participating in community events.

- Educating Consumers: Events and Ceremonies to educate and engage consumers (such as preplanning, estate planning).

- Third-party Marketing: Sales of preplanning services by third-party providers.

- Customer Relationship Management (CRM): Building and maintaining relationships electronically before, during, and after services are rendered.

- Pricing Strategy: For all products and services.

- Sales process when meeting with families.

The Purpose of Advertising

As a radio broadcaster for more than 25 years, one of leading experts in advertising that influenced radio advertising sales across America in the 1990s and 2000s was Michael Corbett. His book, *The 33 Ruthless Rules of Local Advertising*, was written for small retail business owners (like funeral homes) to use advertising money wisely for maximum profitability. In it, he pens, "The purpose of advertising is to create an equity position in a target market (Ideal Consumer) and to reach and motivate a sufficient number of consumers (a critical mass) so that a business can realize a specific growth objective" (Corbett, 1999). Businesses who took his advice saw real results using radio.

Here is a list of advertising tasks and topics that establishes differentiation between marketing and advertising. In advertising, you are:

- Creating content for advertising purposes: Designing and writing ads that communicate what makes your funeral home unique. The copy should "fit" the Funeral Home Type and target Ideal Consumers.

- Media planning: What media type do you use? Meta Platforms? Radio, TV, print, outdoor?

- Post and Boost on Meta Platforms / Facebook and Instagram.

- Media buying: Buying media from trusted, local partners.

- Digital advertising: Google AdWords and SEO.

- Buying advertising to promote ceremonies, events, and education.

As we continue our roadmap, I'm excited about the next chapter, How to Grow Your Business. Did you know there are only four ways to grow a business?

Key Thoughts from Chapter 11:

1. The words "marketing" and "advertising" are mistakenly used interchangeably. That's confusing.

2. Reducing confusion is crucial for strategic progress.

3. "Marketing" is a broad strategy that includes market research, product or service design, audience targeting (your Ideal Consumer), and brand building.

4. "Advertising" is creating content, media planning and buying, digital advertising, and buying advertising to educate and inform consumers.

NOTE: One of my worksheets in Reference 2 at the end of the book will help define who you are, what you stand for, and the competitive landscape in your market.

CHAPTER TWELVE

How Do You Grow a Business?

What kind of *business* do you have? Is your business growing or declining? It's one or the other. Since we're building a Marketing Roadmap for Growing Market Share and Revenue, then like any roadmap, we need a place to start. Knowing where you're starting from provides clarity and makes it easier to set realistic goals and marketing plans or advertising campaigns to achieve them. Additionally, with a clear starting point, you can concentrate your efforts more effectively, and avoid distractions or detours.

Full disclosure: I'm not an accountant and I'm not a financial analyst, but I am a business owner and I have managed plenty of businesses, so from that perspective we have something in common. If you asked me to evaluate your business based on your financials, I would be looking for a 3-to-5-year historical view. Since this book was written in 2024, and COVID dominated at least two of those years, I would recommend a five-year snap-shot. What I would be graphing out is three annual numbers:

- Line 1: Total annual call or case volume per year for the last five years.
- Line 2: Total annual cremation rate per year for the last five years.
- Line 3: Total annual cash flow as a percentage of revenue for the last five years.

Line 1 tells you what kind of business you have. Is it growing or declining? And even though I don't know you and I don't know your business, I'm forecasting Line 2 to be trending up, and that Line 3 to be trending down. And if you were to project out Line 2 over the next five years, I would make another forecast: your projection would show Line 2, the cremation rate, continuing to rise, and Line 3, annual cash flow as a percentage of revenue, is either flat or continuing to shrink.

Are you content with what you see? Are you satisfied? Happy? If you are, super fantastic. Don't stop. Keep going. But if you want to continue expanding, OR if you see something that's disconcerting, making you uncomfortable, are you compelled to do something about it? Establish a growth objective? Make a change?

"Change Occurs When the Pain of Change is Less Than the Pain of Staying the Same."

Here's a good business rule that makes a lot of sense: "Change occurs when the pain of change is less than the pain of staying the same." If you're going to make a change for the purpose of positively affecting your cash flow, then consider a change in your marketing. That's something you *can* control. And keep in mind, the change you make doesn't have to break everything. To the contrary. The change you bring may be simple or subtle. The key begins in this chapter and shows you the four strategies to grow your business. The growth strategies are:

Strategy 1	Strategy 3
Sell more *existing* products and services to *existing* customers.	Sell more *existing* products and services to *new* customers.
Strategy 2	Strategy 4
Sell more *new* products and services to *existing* customers.	Sell more *new* products and services to *new* customers.

That's it. Simple and clear. Growth Strategy 1 is the easiest. These can be customers in Phase 4 of The Journey – Action who are making arrangements and in the process of buying services and merchandise. They can also be in Phase 5 – Retention as future buyers. Strategy 1 would be driven by internal marketing.

Growth Strategy 2 is a little harder. You're still marketing internally, you're still focused on existing customers, but you're introducing new products and services. If you've seen a big trend in the funeral industry over the last 10 years, it's new products and merchandise. From casket liners and blankets to cremation stones and keepsakes, there's a growing list of vendors anxious to offer new ideas to help you sell more and make more. New services should be considered, too.

Growth Strategies 3 and 4 focus on consumers you don't know yet, and they don't know you. They would be considered if you wanted to grow a broader customer base and decided to advertise and reach the right number of Ideal Consumers in Phases 1, 2, and 3 of The Consumer's Journey.

In thinking through this graphic containing the four growth strategies, you can also look at them like this, where Strategies 1 and 2 are based on marketing to existing customers, while Strategies 3 and 4 are based on advertising to new customers:

Marketing	Advertising
Strategy 1 Sell more *existing* products and services to *existing* customers.	**Strategy 3** Sell more *existing* products and services to *new* customers.
Strategy 2 Sell more *new* products and services to *existing* customers.	**Strategy 4** Sell more *new* products and services to *new* customers.

Operational Leverage or Scaling Your Business

Operational leverage occurs when you can generate more revenue from each additional sale because your fixed costs remain constant while variable costs are minimized. Once your fixed costs are covered, then additional sales disproportionately increase profitability. Said another way, if you could scale the business by growing market share and revenue, it's ultimately what you're aiming for, and that's to expand revenue at a faster rate than costs.

Clarity: Putting the Puzzle Pieces Together.

I am excited that you are reading and finishing this chapter. That's because all the pieces we needed to build out a roadmap to achieve a growth objective are in place. You know The Consumer's Journey to Purchasing Funeral Services, you know the five phases they go through (Awareness, Interest, Desire, Action, and Retention), you know the Funeral Buyer Types, you know what Funeral Home Type you are, and now you know the four growth strategies. Let's grow your business.

Key Thoughts from Chapter 12:

1. There are two kinds of businesses: growing or declining.

2. Chances are Line 2, the annual cremation rate, is growing and Line 3, annual cash flow as a percentage of revenue, is trending down.

3. Change occurs when the pain of change is less than the pain of staying the same.

4. Change doesn't have to break everything. Change can be simple or subtle.

5. There are only four growth strategies to grow any business.

6. Reaching existing customers in Phase 5 – Retention requires internal marketing.

7. Reaching new customers in Phases 1, 2, and 3 requires external advertising.

8. Operational leverage occurs when you can generate more revenue from each additional sale because your fixed costs remain constant while variable costs are minimized.

CHAPTER THIRTEEN

How Advertising Works

As you know, one of the largest vendor types in the funeral industry is marketing firms selling pre-need insurance policies. Since they provide such a vital service to so many funeral homes, it's important to provide clarity. You need to know the difference between what they do and the type of marketing and advertising this book is based on.

Direct Marketing

The focus of Direct Marketing would begin with Phase 3 of The Consumer's Journey to Purchasing Funeral Services – Desire. It is a short-term strategy. The main goal of direct marketing is to elicit a direct response from a target audience. An attractive attribute is that it is measurable. That's because when the money is spent, marketers will want to know the result so that an ROI can be calculated. A direct response can be an Immediate At-Need

Funeral Buyer Type, but the primary focus for marketing firms is the Planner. That's because they operate and make profits from commissions earned from the sale of pre-need insurance contracts.

Direct marketing uses more of a direct and straightforward communication style, sometimes personalized to an individual recipient with direct mail or CRM databases. It includes a clear, call-to-action (CTA) and designed to prompt an immediate response. Direct mail is a reliable tool for promoting preplanning events as described in a later chapter. Their CTA is to "reserve your seat" and "enjoy a delicious meal" from our favorite restaurant. It's a proven strategy that gives marketers the opportunity to get leads and make appointments.

Direct marketing is also heavily used in online activities. It can range from preplanning websites to highly targeted campaigns using Google AdWords or Facebook forms to get names, email addresses, and phone numbers. A key thought in all direct marketing endeavors is they are measurable. You can immediately tell if they are effective. Tangible results such as number of responses, leads generated, and conversion rates all funnel into ROI calculations. The direct nature of feedback and results allows for quick adjustments to improve performance.

Brand Advertising's Impact Begins in Phase 1 – Awareness

Brand Advertising's impact would begin with Phase 1 – Awareness. It is a long-term strategy reaching a broad group of consumers (people you don't know, and they don't know you) for the purpose of achieving your growth objectives. How many consumers you are reaching is vitally important and explained in a later chapter.

Brand advertising builds awareness and interest (Phases 1 and 2), provides a positive image, and establishes an equity position in the mind of an Ideal Consumer as described in the next chapter. Branding ads for funeral homes can be written using topics that relieve tension and create trust using The Informative Advertising Style using real people. They also work in creating an emotional connection, brand recognition, and for consumers they may already know, loyalty.

Key thought: It stands to reason that The Premier Funeral Home that's also a marketing and advertising Leader will enjoy better results from direct marketing campaigns because their brand will be more recognizable and trusted. ROI will be better. Conversely, and based on market conditions, a Plateaued funeral home with an Essentialist style may generate early sales but limited from long-term success because other firms in the market have better brand awareness and, perceptually, are considered more trustworthy.

Success is measured over a longer period with the goal of realizing operational leverage. IT REQUIRES PATIENCE. For many, it's harder to quantify, which is a convenient argument to not engage in advertising. Getting results in advertising has always been a challenge for local retail customers. It's even more challenging for funeral homes because of inherent advertising myths in the industry that act as roadblocks. Some of my favorites:

- "Advertising doesn't work for me." Whenever I hear this, the next sentence is always, "Word of mouth is the best form of advertising for me." Well, of course it is. It's also the slowest and most expensive. GEICO or Coca-Cola prove advertising works. This chapter will begin to show how yours can work, too.

- "I don't want to appear opportunistic or sound like a vulture." In my seminars I show a print ad by one of America's leading life insurance providers. It depicts a grandfather hugging a granddaughter, and the headline reads, "Leave love, not stress." Within the copy of the ad it says, "Make sure your loved ones have one less thing to worry about if you're gone." So what's grandpa leaving? Where's grandpa going? Precisely. This big, credible insurance provider is contemplating grandpa's death. Bottom line, if they can advertise a death benefit, you can advertise the benefit of serving a family when they absolutely need it the most.

- "I don't advertise because I don't know what to say." You'll begin to know what to say and how to say it in an upcoming chapter.

Brand Advertising works when you use the Four Pillars of Local Advertising as a rule. What happens far too often is a business will engage in an advertising campaign, but for some reason it didn't work. Most likely it didn't work because one or more of the Four Pillars was missing. It's like a chair. It needs four legs to work. Remove one of the legs and the chair doesn't work. Neither will your advertising.

The Four Pillars of Effective Local Advertising

This secret was explained to me a few years prior to leaving the radio industry. Before I learned it, I was guessing on my advertising and marketing suggestions for my customers. After I learned it and I began applying it, I saw customers getting advertising results. And let me tell you, if you can get results for customers on radio, then you can get results for anyone using The Four Pillars. It's what we use at Post and Boost for all our Facebook, radio, and cable television clients. You can, too. The Four Pillars are:

- **Reach**. How many Ideal Consumers do you reach in a week, a month, or a year? In the funeral industry, it's vitally important that you know how many consumers you need to reach every month to establish a large enough audience in the Awareness and Interest phases. The CDC death rate for the US is instructional here. It's 832 per 100,000 people. If the target market is adults 35+, that essentially cuts the population in half. Our website has a calculator that can help you determine this number (www.postandboost.com/reach). Knowing your number is key. For example, if your firm was doing 250 calls per year, and you wanted to grow by 20%, then you would need to consistently reach 18-21,000 Ideal Consumers per month. You'll learn more in Chapter 16.

- **Frequency**. How many times should your advertising be seen, heard, or read in a 30-day period? If you were a furniture store or car dealer, it would be 3-6 times a week, but for funeral homes it should be less. The numbers we like for frequency are 7-10 times a month for mass media (radio and cable television), and 4-6 times a month for Facebook and Instagram.

- **Consistency**. Funeral homes are always open. That means you should always be advertising. Frequency and consistency are vitally important to establishing something that's familiar. When familiar becomes normal, and normal can be trusted, that's when the possibilities of being the only and obvious choice are greatly improved.

- **Copy**. This is the pillar that must be fed, yet it's the part that most fail at, especially funeral homes. Fresh copy keeps an audience interested and engaged. It also prevents ad fatigue, where consumers start simultaneously ignoring an ad because they have seen it or heard the same ad before. Changing copy on a regular basis ensures advertising remains relevant and resonates to the Ideal Consumer. For Meta Platforms and Facebook, we post and boost ads with new copy and images three times per week. For cable television, we recommend rotating 3-6 ads annually. For radio, after an ad runs 40 times on one radio station, the copy should be changed. Electronic billboards should host 2-4 ad ideas and be changed monthly.

By using the Four Pillars, you are influencing the minds of your Ideal Consumers throughout their Journey. The next chapter, Who Are Your Ideal Consumers, will help you to begin visualizing your audience's "thinking patterns" so that your advertising reaches the right audience.

Repetition and the Illusory Truth Effect

The *illusory truth effect* was discovered by Lynn Hasher, David Goldstein, and Thomas Toppino in 1977. They found that repeated statements were judged more truthful than statements made less frequently, which illustrates how repetition can influence belief and perceived truthfulness (Lynn Hasher, 1977). And if repetition and consistency are keys to establishing trust, if the consumer is now seeing your marketing and advertising on a regular basis and that is normal, their mind will begin to recognize your firm, and, as we'll explain in Chapter 16, Advertising in a Certain Way, you and your people.

"Repetition Builds Trust"

The key to changing the way someone thinks is using the power of repetition. Repetition facilitates learning. Repetition builds trust. Repetition strengthens brand awareness. Repetition reinforces messaging and repetition counters a natural tendency to forget over time. I am being repetitive for one simple reason: Advertisers who think they are being repetitive and stop advertising are making a huge mistake. Remember, what I think and what you think are not as important as what a consumer thinks. If you think your message has been told ad infinitum, it may actually be at a moment when your Ideal Consumer, someone who has been exposed to all of those ads, is consciously watching, listening, reading, and purposefully remembering your funeral home's advertising *for the very first time*. It's breaking through.

My best example of why it would be a mistake to stop advertising comes from my days as a radio broadcaster. Before automation, "DJs" were playing records and announcing live 24-hours a day. When a new hit came out, it could play 12-24 times a day, which means a DJ would play it on their show 3-5 times every day. After a month or so, do you think the DJs were sick of hearing it? Yes. Did they want to stop playing it? Yes. But guess what? That's EXACTLY the amount of time it would take for the new hit, if it is a hit, to get traction with listeners. If I took the DJ's advice and played something else, would we be giving the listeners what they wanted? No. Would our competition be taking our listeners away because they were playing the new hit and we were not? Yes.

You are not the audience. The consumer is. Do The Four Pillars. If you are changing your copy, you are achieving the desired effect, and in this case, it's building trust.

Key Thoughts from Chapter 13:

1. Direct marketing is a short-term strategy that elicits a direct response from a target audience.

2. Brand advertising is a long-term strategy reaching a broad group of consumers (people you don't know, and they don't know you) for the purpose of achieving your growth objectives.

3. The secret to successful brand advertising is using The Four Pillars of Effective Local Advertising.

4. Pillar 1 is Reach. You need to reach enough Ideal Consumers to establish a large enough audience in the Interest phase.

5. Pillar 2 is Frequency. Your advertising needs to be heard enough times to have an impact on growing market share and revenue.

6. Pillar 3 is Consistency. When familiar becomes normal, and normal can be trusted, that's when the chances of being the only and obvious choice are greatly improved.

7. Pillar 4 is Copy. Fresh copy prevents ad fatigue, where consumers start simultaneously ignoring an ad because they have seen it or heard it too often.

8. The Illusory Truth Effect found that repeated statements were judged more truthful than statements made less frequently.

FOURTEEN

Who Are Your Ideal Consumers?

What is the difference between a good revenue year and a great cash flow year? It could be based on serving a few more Ideal Consumers a month, a few more new customers, or maybe customers who just happen to purchase a lot of services that results in your realizing operational leverage. The good news could mean your marketing and advertising doesn't have to change the thought processes of the entire market. No. That would be too expensive. Instead, can you change or convert just a few *Ideal Consumers*, or as Seth Godin describes it, "the smallest viable market"? (Godin, 2018)

To get to that place, and to identify the Ideal Consumers who would make up your smallest viable market, it's important to know who you are and what you stand for. What is your Funeral Home Type and the Funeral Buyer Types that on the surface seem to fit? How do their thinking patterns match? And referencing the last chapter, this might be based on Growth Strategy 3, selling more existing products and services to new customers.

Narrating Your Ideal Consumer

Try this. Narrate a description of your ideal customer. For example, if you're a Premier Funeral Home, it could read something like this: "Our ideal customer is someone we don't know yet, is an at-need or preplanning man or a woman over the age of 65 who has lived in our community for more than five years. They are religious, attend church, own their homes, have children and grandchildren, are on solid financial footing, and physically live within 10 miles of our funeral home."

If that was your ideal customer, can you imagine what that person looks like? Would it be easier to recognize them if you saw them? If you had 30 seconds to introduce you and your firm, like with an "elevator pitch," what would you say that would make them curious? Want to get to know you? If you're using Growth Strategy 3, selling more existing products and services to new customers, would it require some form of external marketing? Would it be on Facebook? Radio? Television? Billboards? And where do these people congregate? Where do they gather? Have they ever attended a funeral at your funeral home? Do they know someone that you know? Instead of marketing directly to them, could you passively market to them with events or ceremonies? A preplanning seminar? A sunrise service? A workshop featuring a lawyer offering estate planning and will creating? Maybe an open house? Are there community events you leverage that they already participate in? An annual parade? Movie nights?

Yes, there are many variables and lots of ideas, but that's the point. By knowing your ideal customer, developing a marketing plan that includes external advertising can be created.

Let's try it again. If you are an Emerging Funeral Home, one of your Ideal Consumers could look like this: "Our Ideal Consumer is someone we don't know and is an at-need man or a woman between the ages of 50 and 65 with a new-to-town persona who has lived in our community for less than five years. They may or may not be religious, and since they are new here may not be in a church family, they may own a home or are still living in temporary housing, they may have kids but not grandchildren, their financial stability is not a priority, and they live within 15 miles of the funeral home."

Can You See Your Ideal Consumer?

If that was your ideal customer, just like the first example, can you see them? Could you recognize them if you had to? Obviously, your marketing strategies and external advertising will clearly be different. For example, your strategy could be to establish a key funeral director or owner as a trusted spokesperson. Using radio stations that reach this crowd with well-scripted ads appealing to consumers in Phases 1 and 2 of the Consumer's Journey may be on target. Facebook and Instagram posts of their face make sense. A Welcome Wagon sponsorship would also be good. Community events might be different, too. Sponsoring or participating in an annual 5 or 10K race, food festival, Veterans Day BBQ, anything where someone new in the community would go and gather, are all good ideas. You could even offer FREE calendars and other giveaways with the funeral home name, logo, and phone number that would benefit someone new to your community.

You Can't Serve Everyone

You can't serve everyone, and you can't change the way everyone thinks, but what you can do is identify the people you can serve, your Ideal Consumers, the ones that would be the most receptive to your marketing. Focus on them. Ignore the rest. Doing it correctly could make the difference between a good revenue year and a great cash flow year because you were able to successfully achieve operational leverage.

Key Thoughts from Chapter 14:

1. The difference between a good revenue year and a great cash flow year could be just a few more Ideal Consumers.

2. Ideal Consumers will make up your smallest, viable market.

3. To identify the smallest viable market, you start with knowing who you are and what you stand for.

4. By knowing your Ideal Consumers, developing a marketing plan that includes external advertising can be created.

5. You can't serve everyone, and you can't change the way everyone thinks, but what you can do is identify the people you can serve, your ideal customer.

NOTE: One of my worksheets in Reference 2 at the end of the book will help you define your Ideal Consumers.

CHAPTER FIFTEEN

What Media Do You Use?

You can't serve everyone, and you can't change the way everyone thinks, but what you can do is use The Four Pillars of Effective Local Advertising and, starting from your smallest viable market, grow from there. In this chapter we want to help you choose the media that lets you efficiently and effectively do that.

First, I would like to recognize the people dynamics of a marketing area. If you are a decision maker at your firm, you are going to have salespeople calling on you to sell advertising. They represent either locally/regionally owned or corporate-owned media, and so you know, what's happened to funeral homes has also happened to television and radio broadcasting. Many regional or major market stations are owned by national corporations.

The salespeople calling on you are representing they have viewers, listeners, or readers, and you're giving them money to reach them for you. The first thing you should understand is, in most cases, these people are trying to sell time or space. It's rare that a media representative understands how advertising works, the funeral industry, what to say in funeral advertising, and ultimately how to get you the results you are looking for. For them it's not the message; it's the media. And what's going to be confusing to you is knowing whether or not they are really representing enough viewers, listeners, or readers who also happen to be your Ideal Consumers. Funeral homes serve neighborhoods and communities. So does the media.

The Newspaper is No Longer a Viable Medium.

Second, the mass media landscape has dramatically changed in the last 15-20 years. It began with two significant milestones: In 2006, Facebook started enrolling members 13 years of age or older with a valid email address. Then, in 2007, the Time Magazine invention of the year was the iPhone. What's remarkable is that the newspaper industry, which began in April 1704 with "The Boston News-Letter" and was the dominant media through the early 2000's, lost the majority of their readers to Facebook. Today, the newspaper is no longer a viable medium.

Radio and television broadcasters are struggling to maintain market share, too. For radio, as an example, the number of choices on the FM dial has exploded. The FCC has given FM licenses to AM radio stations because consumers have left the AM dial. Add to that the ability to receive Class C stations from as far as 50 miles away, the reality is listeners have too many choices. What makes it even worse is the big music stations are losing market share. First it was to satellite providers, but that was at a cost to consumers. Now, they can use their hand-held electronic devices and download apps that dynamically create personalized playlists. And for many, it's either free or they're willing to pay a monthly fee.

TV broadcasters are also transitioning. HD technology forced on them by the FCC has improved over-the-air (OTA) technology. One benefit was to give consumers more choices, and there is a growing number of consumers buying antennas as part of adopting Next Gen TV. But the streaming industry is exploding. Again, hand-held electronic devices give consumers too many video choices. Oh, and don't forget cable television providers. They deliver hundreds of channels, too.

To Discover What Works in Mass Media, Follow the Money

How can you tell if a certain medium can work for you? Like anything else, it's based on supply and demand. Don't get me wrong, broadcasters have a robust industry, generate $1.23 trillion in economic activity, and in 2024 provided more than 2.5 million jobs (Broadcasters, 2024). What you're looking for are the radio and TV stations that consistently command higher prices for their advertising. They can because they work. They have a critical mass of viewers or listeners. They can keep their rates up because there are enough advertising buyers getting results. To discover what works in mass media, follow the money.

There are markets where some mass media outlets can be efficient and effective. Maybe you have a regional firm with multiple locations, and you cover a radius of 30-60 miles. Regional TV and radio would make sense if you broke the cost down by location. You could also be a stand-alone in a community where certain stations continue to attract a critical mass of Ideal Consumers who are their viewers or listeners.

Another factor to consider is the broadcast coverage area. Does the physical coverage area mirror your actual area of service (optimal), or does it reach a bigger area, meaning that a part of your advertising cost is always wasted?

Meta Platforms is a Dominant Media in Your Market

I have invested space in this chapter to place weight on the dynamics of local media and the people who own and operate them for one reason. Perception. They have salespeople who have local branding, they have market history, they can take you to lunch, give airtime and money to your favorite causes, and they have a physical presence. But guess what? There is not one local television station, one local radio station, or one local newspaper in your market bigger than Meta Platforms. You just don't know it because they haven't sent a salesperson to knock on your door. Yet. And to be sure you know, Meta Platforms owns the social media apps Facebook, Instagram, and WhatsApp.

According to Pew Research, apart from YouTube, no other social media platform comes close to Facebook in usage. The report relays that around seven in ten US adults (68%) use Facebook, a percentage that has been consistent since 2016. The report goes on to say that roughly half of adults (47%) report using Instagram (Schaeffer, 2024).

Meta Platforms (Facebook and Instagram) is Effective and Efficient

One of the immediate benefits of direct marketing is how it is measurable. Brand advertising on Facebook with Meta Platforms is measurable, too. Mass media is not. Mass media is an "estimate" based on ratings or anecdotal evidence. Translated, anecdotal evidence can also mean no evidence. And unlike mass media where audiences are based on the physical location of a tower and transmitter, Meta Platforms lets you geofence an audience to within one mile. That's efficient, especially if you have a definable service area. How many consumers do you need to change? That's covered in the next chapter.

Creating Audiences on Meta Platforms to Target Your Ideal Consumers

In mass media, targeting a demographic is accomplished by radio formats or television programming, which is inexact at best. It means you're paying for advertising to consumers that are not your Ideal Consumers. With Facebook, your audience can be based on a specific age, gender, location, and interest. For example:

- If there was an area within the community you serve with a high likelihood of Ideal Consumers, Facebook can target them by zip code, or a radius as small as one mile. For branding topics, you may choose an audience of adults 35+.

- For preplanning, an audience of adults 55+ that is also interested in retirement communities, financial planning, health and fitness, and life insurance.

- To reach people who may have preplanned with another firm, you could advertise to the same preplanning audience, but exclude users who "like" your business page.

- If you own a Price Strategy Funeral Home, your audience will have an interest in coupons, discount stores, and deals of the day.

- For funeral homes targeting veterans, your audience can be adults 45+ who are interested in Memorial Day, Veterans Day, The United States Veterans Administration, and military history.

- For the innovator funeral homes promoting direct cremation or green care, your audience can be interested in climate, renewable energy, or ecology.

- Specialty Funeral Homes can build an audience based on interests in faith-based topics or music targeting cultures.

Meta Platforms Costs are Far Less Than Mass Media

If you're buying broadcast television, you should budget anywhere from $2,000 to $8,000 a month. Small market radio can be $300 to $800 per month, but the real cost may actually be high because the small market radio station may only have 1,000-2,000 Ideal Consumers. Depending on your market and scheduling, regional radio will be $2,000-$8,000 a month. Major metros, more.

Facebook costs are far less than mass media. At Post and Boost, we see the cost per thousand to be on average between $5 and $9. A $500 monthly budget can reach 15,000-25,000 consumers 3-6 times (50,000 – 75,000 impressions). Very efficient! Plus, your competitors will have no sense you are investing advertising dollars on Facebook. We call it the Quiet Storm, where you know exactly what you're doing, but your competitors don't.

Advertising Purchased Using the Meta Business Suite Appears on Instagram

Advertisers are interested in Instagram for a good reason. Yes, it's a younger demographic, but they're not all young. Buying advertising using the Meta Business Suite is reaching users based on the chosen audience. The Ads Manager can place them anywhere to achieve the most efficient buy possible. That means Meta Business Suite ads will be seen both on Facebook and Instagram.

What Media Should You Use?

Here is a simple foundational guide to consider:

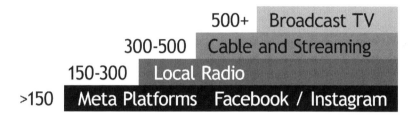

The numbers on the left represent call or case volume. What this is suggesting is for any funeral home, Meta Platforms is efficient from a cost perspective, and effective in achieving the kind of reach and frequency you would need to accomplish a growth objective. If you're doing more than 150, consider adding local radio. For 300 – 500, a mix of Meta Platforms, local radio, and cable would be strong. Adding broadcast TV or regional radio doing 500 or more calls would be something a Leader would do.

The next chapter is about doing the math and calculating how many consumers you need to change to achieve a growth objective. It also introduces the idea of focusing on the smallest viable market when creating audiences for campaigns.

Key Thoughts from Chapter 15:

1. By and large, most media representatives are trying to sell time and space.

2. The mass media landscape has dramatically changed in the last 20 years because of the start of Facebook in 2006, and the Time Magazine 2007 invention of the year, the iPhone.

3. The newspaper is no longer a viable medium.

4. Broadcast Radio and TV stations (mass media) are struggling to maintain market share.

5. To discover the mass media that works in your market, follow the money.

6. No social media platform other than YouTube comes close to Facebook in usage. Instagram is right behind it. Meta Platforms own both.

7. Brand advertising and direct marketing with Meta Platforms is measurable.

8. You can create audiences on Meta Platforms to reach your Ideal Consumers.

9. Facebook costs are far less than mass media.

10. Advertising on Meta Business Suite also appears on Instagram. You get both.

NOTE: One of my worksheets in Reference 2 at the end of the book will help you conceptualize and create campaigns.

SIXTEEN

How Many Consumers Do You Need to Change?

Clearly in the last chapter I presented Meta Platforms as a must-use medium. It's easy, best, and logical because, from The Four Pillars perspective, it's straightforward to implement, from a targeted reach perspective, measurable and unbeatable, and from a budgeting perspective, efficient and a good deal. Plus, with a solid boosting budget on Facebook and Instagram (Meta Platforms), not only can it be your primary advertising medium, but you can also be a Leader.

Having said that, then please understand all media works. Radio, television, cable, Facebook and Instagram, outdoor, direct mail, they all work, otherwise they would not be in business.

What Works? And What Doesn't Work?

Two very simple business questions. What works? And what doesn't work? If you can figure out what aspects of your marketing and advertising work, then keep doing it. Conversely, if what you're using doesn't work, cancel it. Use the money on what does work. Use The Four Pillars of Effective Local Advertising to get results.

If it works, do it.

If there is a local radio station that has a lot of Ideal Consumers, use it. If a small station does obituaries and older consumers listen to it, sponsor it. If you feel like you can overwhelm a competitor with broadcast television while reinforcing your Premier position in the market, buy it. If the big, urban radio station gives you the power to establish the history of your firm to retain your customers, advertise on it. If there's a gospel radio station and you're a faith-based Specialty Funeral Home, share your message. The key here is if it works, do it, because whether you knew it or not, whether it was intentional or not, or if you just lucked into it, it's probably following the rules of The Four Pillars.

Establishing a Growth Objective

A "growth objective" is a specific and measurable goal that a business sets to increase its market share, customer base, or revenue over a defined period. It's a foundational objective that measures and guides the strategic direction of your marketing and advertising. Our focus will be to use call or case volume as the baseline, and a new goal as a growth objective. For example, if you're doing 200 calls or cases a year, and now your goal is 250, then 250 is your growth objective. I'm assuming you know what the average margin per call is and compensating for including or excluding direct cremations.

Market Analysis

Let's begin by looking at the market you serve. For the purposes of this book, we are going to establish that the market has a population of 100,000 people. What you probably already know is how many calls or cases there are in your area every year, but if you were to project out a number that can be used globally, we would get there by using the CDC mortality rate, which for 100,000 of the US population in 2023 was 832.8 (Farida B. Ahmas, Jodi A. Cisewski, Jiaquan Xu, & Robert N. Anderson, 2023).

To determine the number of funeral services needed in a market or the market mortality rate, the formula is: Market population multiplied by .832 equals mortality rate. To graph it out:

Population	Mortality Rate
100,000	832
150,000	1,248
200,000	1,664

Working in round numbers, if the market has a population of 100,000, there are approximately 800 to 850 calls or cases in your market in your year. We'll use the 832 number as the baseline. If you are doing 200 calls per year, then your market share is 24%.

Hypothetically, if your growth objective was to grow your call or case volume from 200 calls or cases to 250 calls per year, or 30% market share, then you would need to grow by, on average, one call per week, or four a month.

Are There Enough Ideal Consumers in Your Market to Grow?

If you're doing 200 calls or cases a year, then the other funeral homes in the area you are serving would represent the rest, or 632. Something you already know: If you intend to increase market share, it will be at the expense of another funeral home in your market. That's because, unlike other businesses, you can't "create" death. The number of death calls is finite.

Who Are You Trying to Reach?

If your Ideal Consumer is on the top of your mind, then describe them demographically. For branding your business, and depending on your market size, you may choose to focus on adults 35+. I like that number because in conversations with clients, it's the number they agree with most. With adults 35+ you're reaching the older adults and, if they are in the same community, their adult kids.

According to Neilsberg Research, just under 55% of the US is 35+ (Neilsberg, 2023), so to begin with most adults who represent the market's death calls, that audience would be 55,000. Said another way, if you were to effectively advertise to 55,000 adults in your market (very expensive), you are attempting to persuade, inform, and remind families who will be involved with 832 death calls. That's everybody. But you don't serve everybody.

Focusing On the Smallest Viable Market

If we were to focus on the smallest viable market, the number would be somewhere between 50 and 100. It's one of the reasons that Phase 5 – Retention is a vitally important phase to focus on because it's *working with people that we know.* ***But we don't know most of the people we are trying to change. They don't know us, and we don't know them.***

How Many Adults 35+ Do You Need to Reach?

Hypothetically a firm that's serving 200 families per year (24% market share) would need to consistently reach an estimated 12,000-14,000 adults 35+ per month to maintain market share. That reach estimate is calculated using this formula: Market population multiplied by 55%. The total is then multiplied by a funeral home's market share. Example results:

Population	Adults 35+	24% Market Share
100,000	55,000	13,200
150,000	82,500	19,800
200,000	110,000	24,400

If the growth objective is 250, or 30% market share, then the estimated number of adults you would need to consistently reach would grow to 16,000-18,000 adults 35+ per month. It looks like this:

Population	Adults 35+	30% Market Share
100,000	55,000	16,500
150,000	82,500	24,750
200,000	110,000	33,000

If 16,500 population represents 30% of the market, and you have a 25% share, then theoretically 25% of that number, or 4,100 population could represent the calls you would normally get, which would mean (again theoretically) 12,375 population represents consumers who are not doing business with you. By focusing on the full 16,500 population that represents a growth objective of 250, and by using the Four Pillars, you are reaching enough new consumers enough times in the Awareness, Interest, and Desire phases, and customers of yours who are in the Retention phase, to achieve your growth objective.

In building audiences for your advertising campaigns, there are proven strategies to refine the demographics and psychographics to enhance campaign performance. This involves matching Funeral Buyer Types or thinking patterns with your funeral home. By tailoring your approach, you can more effectively target and engage your Ideal Consumers.

The Preplanning Audience

The preplanning audience has certain interests that can be defined in Facebook. From an age perspective, the other number most of my customers agree with is adults 55+. That would mean if you're advertising preplanning, and that represents 29% of the population, or 29,000 adults 55+, and growth objective is 30% market share, then you would want an estimated reach of 8,000 to 10,000 adults 55+ consistently and effectively every month. See how it works?

Population	Adults 55+	30 % Market Share
100,000	29,000	8,700
150,000	43,500	13,000
200,000	58,000	17,400

In Reference 2, there is a Reach Worksheet that allows you to enter your growth objective numbers to determine the number of adults you need to reach in your market.

How Many Campaigns Do You Need to be Running?

An advertising campaign is a series of coordinated advertisements with a single theme or topic promoting a product or service to a targeted audience. The worksheet in Reference 2 will be helpful as you conceptualize an advertising campaign. Key elements include growth strategy to be used, narration of the Ideal Consumer and thinking patterns to be targeted, budgets, and durations.

If you're advertising to adults 35+ and you're using the Informative Advertising Style that's presented to you in the next chapter, that's one campaign. If you're advertising for preplanning, that's another campaign. You can run more than one campaign. What makes Facebook so logical is it's simply two different ads to two different audiences, and because Facebook is measurable, you can correctly do the math and feel confident you're advertising to enough people to achieve your growth objective. You can also use interests in Facebook to further reduce the size of the audience you need to reach to be even more effective (i.e., focus on the interests that make up your Ideal Consumer and exclude the interests that don't).

Another Way to Look at Radio, Television, and Cable

Some media outlets can give you valid audience estimates. If they are available, use them. Explain to your media representative who your Ideal Consumers are, *where they live*, and how can you best reach them. In radio, Sundays and Mondays have the most open inventory and can be the least expensive. For broadcast television and cable, overnight times are perfect because many older consumers who have difficulty sleeping are watching.

The Cost and the Benefit

For the record, I love cable television and I love radio stations who have enough Ideal Consumers for a funeral home. If your funeral home was doing $2,000,000 in annual sales and your marketing and advertising budget was 5-7%, that would mean you're spending about $10,000 per month, which could easily support Facebook and other media. My experience has been that these percentages, which are low for retail, are high for the funeral industry. At the end of the day, when you consider your growth objectives, you know what is best for you. Considering the cost and the benefit, and your belief that all this will work, decide that your advertising budget is an investment, not a cost. It's a lot easier when you know who you are, you know what you stand for, and you're doing the right things. Be patient. You're expanding your business.

Improving Your Prospects for Success

If you think you're going to take market share from a Premier Funeral Home and their advertising style is one of a Leader, the road to success may be long. However, if their advertising style is Essentialist, then your prospects of success might be better. In either case, you would want to carefully identify the audiences and topics that give you the most opportunity over the next 5-15 years. And, if there is another firm in your market you could identify as Plateaued doing 75-100 calls per year, and their advertising style is an Essentialist, then their tribe or customer base may be vulnerable. Again, you're improving your prospects for success. Ultimately, is there market share that can be changed in your direction?

Does Your Competitor Have a Weakness?

And the other thought here is that some funeral homes may have a weakness that's not perceived by the market, but because you're into it, you're clearly aware of it. One example of a weakness is a firm with some level of pride that has gone too far and has become arrogance. Ad copy can be created to present a warm, trusting, down-to-earth message that authentically connects to a consumer. Another weakness could be stability of staff. The competition has lost some key staff members. Maybe some of them now work for you. Ads can be created for that weakness, too.

For Your Consideration

What do consumers have to say about funeral home advertising? Well, here, there are two kinds of consumers. One type is those who have never been served by a funeral home or are ignorant of the process. Demographically they tend to be younger. These are individuals who are unwilling to understand funerals or the funeral process because on the surface it's icky or mysterious. It's easier to ignore it. Some reject it out of hand. In that crowd, they're the ones on Facebook who bully funeral homes for having the utter gall to advertise in their newsfeed about something that they think should not be advertised. Everyone has an opinion, and on social media, some feel so entitled they habitually pontificate. These are the ones who consistently prove themselves worthy of being ignored and blocked.

The other kind of consumer HAS been served by a funeral home. They get it. They have faced life's toughest moments with a talented and compassionate funeral director surrounded by assistants and staff members that care. As you can imagine, these are older consumers, and these are the Ideal Consumers you want to talk to as they progress along their journey to purchasing funeral services.

The next chapter is about how to advertise in a certain way. It's a style of advertising that is conservative, professional, and consistent with the standards of a funeral home that believes its most valuable asset is its reputation.

Key Thoughts from Chapter 16:

1. All media works if you're using The Four Pillars of Effective Local Advertising.

2. Ask yourself these two questions about your advertising: What works? And what doesn't work? Keep doing the advertising that is working and cancel that advertising that is not.

3. To determine the audience size you need to advertise to, it begins with the CDC US death rate of 832.8 per 100,000 population.

4. For branding campaigns, use adults 35+, which represents just under 55% of the market's population. For preplanning campaigns, use adults 55+, which represents 29% of the population.

5. Establish a growth objective, then do a market analysis to determine how many adults you need to reach monthly to achieve it.

6. Based on the topics you are using and your growth objectives, you may be running more than one campaign.

7. Improve your prospects for success. If there is no Leader in your market, be one.

8. For your consideration: Ignore the consumer that's never been served by a funeral home or a funeral professional.

NOTE: One of my worksheets in Reference 2 at the end of the book will help you calculate the number of consumers you need to reach to achieve a growth objective.

CHAPTER SEVENTEEN

How to Advertise in a Certain Way

What makes a funeral home unique? As we finished Chapter 10 and talked about what makes a funeral home unique, from a marketing and advertising perspective, a funeral home creates *tension*. The funeral home that successfully relieves tension in the mind of the consumer is fundamentally building trust, and without a doubt, trust is a cornerstone of the relationship between a funeral home and its Ideal Consumers. When a funeral home engages in the Four Pillars of Effective Local Advertising and consistently demonstrates through its advertising that it can relieve the stress and anxiety associated with a funeral home, it's on the way to earning trust.

How do you advertise in a certain way? And what does "a certain way" mean? Wallace Wattles in his timeless classic, *The Science of Getting Rich*, phrases it like this: "When two men (funeral homes) in the same business are in the same neighborhood, and one gets rich while the other fails, it indicates that getting rich is the result of doing things in a *certain way*" (Wattles, 1910).

The Informative Advertising Style

Even though funeral homes are B2C, local retail businesses, their advertising must be different from furniture stores, car dealers, or sub sandwich shops. It's why this chapter suggests a style that allows you to advertise in a certain way. It's called, "The Informative Advertising Style."

The Informative Advertising Style is most effective when it uses real people to educate and inform consumers traveling through The Consumer's Journey of Purchasing Funeral Services using a variety of media. It's not catchy, doesn't "breakthrough" like the examples in Chapter 1, never uses cliché, completely avoids humor, and never makes sales claims. What it does do is achieve trust through consistent, topic-based content that relates to the funeral home, the funeral process, or the benefits of preplanning. It's a style that builds a relationship with Ideal Consumers through reliable, helpful information and education, and positions the funeral home as a knowledgeable and trustworthy authority.

Creating advertising that relieves tension involves focusing on empathetic, trustworthy messaging. The "talent," the faces and the voices used in the Informative Advertising Style are real people and is best when they are actual leaders or employees with a deep connection to the business. The backdrop or the "scene" is the funeral home itself. Written copy should convey warmth, understanding, and a sense of comfort and support during difficult times. By using real people that emphasize compassionate and professional care, incorporating an Informative

Advertising Style can begin to relieve the perceived tension of a funeral home.

Using real people in funeral home advertisements can significantly enhance the effectiveness of its marketing and advertising.

In my early days of writing Facebook advertising for funeral homes, it was Jim Lowe of Lowe Funeral Home and Crematory in Burlington NC who gave me a crucial insight that helped shape the Informative Advertising Style. When I asked Jim what he thought made his funeral home unique, without hesitation he said, "Our people. It's our people that make Lowe Funeral Home unique." Inspired by this, I began taking pictures of people everywhere in the funeral home. People standing in front of the building next to the sign, assistants next to lecterns or opening doors, funeral directors in visitation rooms or where they arrange funerals with families, even office administrators where they do their work.

It was what we saw on Facebook during these early days of posting and boosting authentic pictures of real people that has become a guiding principle in our business, Post and Boost, Inc., and the cornerstone of the Informative Advertising Style. We saw first-hand how consumers organically reacted to real people on Facebook. It mirrored a perfectly controlled focus group. Consumers were enthusiastically engaging in our Facebook advertising. It was resonating. They were commenting on staff members with the kind of celebration and recognition that can only be given to special, compassionate people.

That's the answer. The consumer told us that real people on Facebook work. It's also the reason we feature real people on radio and television ads. And as I give credit to the consumer and how they interact with today's advertising on Facebook, I can confidently say *what I think or what you think is not nearly as important as what a consumer thinks*, and we heard them loud and clear.

The Benefits of Using Real People

Seeing actual faces associated with a funeral home fosters a more personal and meaningful connection, and by doing so relieves tension. When consumers recognize that there are real, approachable, and professional people behind the services it's advertising, it humanizes the brand and builds trust. When consumers can see the faces of the real people who will be directly involved with arranging and conducting services, it makes the advertising relatable. It also gives them the information they need to visualize their own interactions at the funeral home. If they can see themselves being comforted and supported by these real people, that can be a deciding factor that makes your funeral home the only and obvious choice.

The Four Pillars of Effective Local Advertising

The Informative Advertising Style is reliant on The Four Pillars of Effective Local Advertising – reach, frequency, consistency, and copy. To be successful, the advertising should consistently reach enough prospective customers to support your growth objective enough times (frequency) with always changing copy. In the radio business, the phrase we always shared with each other and customers to emphasize the goal of using The Four Pillars was to "persuade, inform, and remind."

Topics Are a Form of Education and Information

Topics serve as the subjects or themes education and information can be based on or revolve around. They provide the foundation for content, plus help organize and focus the information in a way that is more relevant to the Ideal Consumer. Topics are also far easier to write. Here are example topics, including some that are expanded on in the next chapter:

- **Facility**. Consumers should see pictures of staff members in chapels, foyers, and in front of your facility. If your funeral home is beautiful, it's an asset that should be leveraged. Written copy can convey beauty, a place of peace, and where families gather to tell stories, share hugs, and begin their journey of healing. Visuals play a role in relieving tension because if a consumer regularly sees what the inside of your funeral home looks like, it's reducing one of the fear factors.

- **Branding Funeral Directors**. Funeral directors perform a valuable service. Explain to consumers what they do. Authentic images of funeral directors on Facebook or as spokespeople in radio or television ads are effective, especially in TV ads that also show your facility. Copy can include asking and answering hypothetical questions, expressing pride in their work, and explaining to consumers how they love to serve families. Remember, if marketing is solving a problem, the funeral director perceptually has the most experience.

- **Educating the consumer**. As described in the next chapter.

- **Preplanning**. Easily the most popular topic that fits an informative style. Preplanning ads should convey the obvious benefits to preplanning a funeral, as well as making the call-to-action easy and clear.

- **Cremation options**. This is a topic that emphasizes how most consumers know what cremation is but not much more. The consumer has many options that can certainly lead to the funeral home providing more services. The call-to-action should include meeting with a funeral director to discover the options best for the family.

- **Veterans**. Although this topic is directed to Veterans, it gives the funeral home the opportunity to thank them for their service. The services provided are special, meaningful, and traditional.

- **Team Process**. This is a topic that helps the consumer understand the funeral home's commitment to service by always being available, always ready to serve as a team.

This is my writing style for advertising on Facebook, radio, or television, The Informative Advertising Style. The topics resonate because they are relevant to funeral consumers. I like to feel like my ads are well-crafted, straightforward, almost utilitarian, practical, and easy to understand. The tone and manner, whether written or spoken aloud with the correct music, acknowledges the emotional state of the consumer, and that the funeral home is a compassionate partner to help solve a problem. It's why we use real people. And for funeral homes adhering to The Four Pillars of Effective Local Advertising, The Informative Advertising Style makes it easier for consumers to see they are the only and obvious choice.

Education is not only a topic, but it also plays a key role in relieving tension. That's what Chapter 18 is all about.

Key Thoughts from Chapter 17:

1. The funeral home that successfully relieves tension in the mind of the consumer is fundamentally building trust.

2. The Informative Advertising Style is a style that allows funeral homes to advertise in a certain way.

3. The Informative Advertising Style achieves trust through consistent, topic-based content that relates to the funeral home, the funeral process, or the benefits of preplanning.

4. Using real people in funeral home advertisements can significantly enhance the effectiveness of its marketing and advertising.

5. The Informative Advertising Style is reliant on The Four Pillars of Effective Local Advertising to get results.

6. Topics serve as subjects or themes that information can be based on or revolve around.

7. When writing copy for ads, topics are far easier to write.

CHAPTER EIGHTEEN

Educating and Informing the Consumer

If funeral homes create tension, and according to Seth Godin, "forward motion relieves that tension" (Godin, 2018), then education and information is a preferred form of forward motion for funeral homes. That's because education and information creates a progression from a state of uncertainty and tension to one of understanding and clarity. This is the kind of progression that not only alleviates tension, *but it also builds trust*, and that is a key. As a consumer becomes aware, more informed, and better educated, they can begin to build confidence as they progress through the Desire phase of the Journey. That, in turn, can foster a trusting relationship with a funeral home.

"Matching Consumer Thinking Patterns to Your Funeral Home Type"

A "thinking pattern," as mentioned in the chapter on Funeral Buyer Types, is the habitual way a consumer processes information, makes decisions, and solves problems. In this book, a Funeral Buyer Type and persona is a consumer's thinking pattern. A wise funeral marketer will know how to match desirable Funeral Buyer Types with their Funeral Home Type. If there is a match or fit, then educating and informing consumers would be based on reinforcing obvious thinking patterns or the status quo. If there is not a match, then use education and information as a topic in advertising campaigns to interrupt their thinking patterns. The worksheet offered at the end of book (see Reference 2) , defining your Ideal Consumers using their thinking patterns, will be helpful.

Education and Information Can Significantly Contribute to Creating Trust

After identifying Funeral Buyer Types and Funeral Home Types in Chapters 8 and 9, did you begin to see who you are and what you stand for in a different way? If that's clear, then what should also be clear is the Buyer Types you want to attract to your funeral home to expand your business. Repeating how we finished Chapter 10, Funeral Home Types, you're in a business that most consumers have little prior knowledge or experience of until the need arises (Phase 3 – Desire). *Education and information can significantly contribute to creating trust.* By providing clear, helpful, trust-building education and information in Phases 1 and 2 of the Consumer's Journey, they may feel more confident and secure when they enter Phase 4 and decide your funeral home is the only and obvious choice.

"Matching Educational and Informational Topics"

Matching educational and informational topics to your Funeral Home and desirable Buyer Types should be a thoughtful and thorough process. Think it through. Take your time. There could be more than one. You know your funeral home better than anyone else, and you know you. You are the driver. You are the one that will start this process and create change in your market. How many people will you change? Convert to your way of thinking? It may only be a few to start, but sometimes the key to a successful year is just a few more calls. One of my worksheets in Reference 2 at the end of the book will help you figure this out.

Here are ten examples of educational and informational topics and how they can be associated with Funeral Home and Buyer Types:

How can a preplanned funeral benefit you? Preplanning is one of the leading advertised and marketed services. The objective is to educate consumers on why they should preplan. Benefits can be directed towards the consumer or their family. Funeral Home Types are going to be broad because building a preplan book is desirable to ensure future growth. Types include The Premier, Emerging, Innovative, and Specialty funeral homes. Buyer types include The Preplanner and The Customizer.

Here is a 60-second radio script with a holiday theme that speaks to this: *"As we approach the holiday season and start thinking about the gifts we will give; consider a gift your family will appreciate...forever! This is Bill Johnston, a Funeral Director at Johnston Funeral Home. The gift I'm suggesting isn't wrapped in paper and tied with a bow. The gift I'm suggesting is preplanning your funeral at Johnston Funeral Home. Now, at first glance, some might not see it as the gift of the year. But as the years go by, and when it comes time to celebrate your life, they will realize it was one of most thoughtful gifts you could have ever given them. They'll also be grateful you spared them from the stress and uncertainty of making decisions during an emotional time. To plan or preplan your funeral, or the funeral of a loved one, call us or come see us at Johnston Funeral Home, proud to serve the Daphne area for six generations."*

What happens at your funeral home? Funeral homes create tension, which is why it's vitally important to educate a consumer on what happens and why. Your funeral home is where the journey towards healing can begin. It's where families and friends can physically and emotionally support each other with knowing smiles, tender hugs, and memorable stories that bring joyous laughter or quiet tears. It's what happens at your funeral home every day. This is an ideal topic for The Premier and Emerging Funeral Homes who are Leaders. Buyer Types are The At-Need Buyer, The Preplanner, and The Customizer.

Here's a 60-second radio ad that speaks to this: *"Have you ever stepped inside a funeral home before? This is Bill Johnston, a Funeral Director for Johnston Funeral Home. When people discover who I am and what I do, they're often curious, especially if they've never visited a funeral home before. It's true, there's a kind of quiet that envelops you when you walk through our doors. But what we hear and what we see at Johnston Funeral Home is deeply gratifying. As families gather to receive friends and celebrate a life, yes… there are tears, but there's also lots of hugs and lots of laughter. And as the deceased is transitioning and everyone is saying their goodbyes, surviving family members are transitioning, too. They're beginning their journey of hope and healing, and by being here, they can see the path forward a little easier. Johnston Funeral Home, 510 West 4th Street, Daphne, the Baldwin County area's oldest family-owned funeral home."*

What does a funeral director do, and how does a funeral director benefit you? Not only does this educational topic give funeral homes plenty to talk about, if done with advertising on Facebook, radio, or television, it can be an effective way to give consumers the opportunity to put a name and a face to the process. Remembering when something is familiar becomes normal, and normal can be trusted, putting funeral directors in the position to educate the public on what their role is makes them approachable. Wouldn't it be far better if a consumer had some kind of relationship with one of your funeral directors so that direct questions could be answered and trust established well before a death? This clearly fits Premier and Emerging Funeral Homes. Buyer types are At-Need (personas can include the caring buyer) and Preplanners (the inspired buyer and the courageous buyer).

Here's a 60-second radio script that speaks to this: *"This is Bill Johnston with Johnston Funeral Home & Crematory, and I am a Funeral Director. I'm proud to live, work, and worship in this community. Over the years I've come to expect how people react when they discover what I do for a living. I usually get one of two reactions. The first is somebody who has never lost someone. They've never been to a funeral home, let alone a funeral. They don't know what to say, so they might cut a cute joke that's cute to them...and that's okay. I get it. Then there's the person who has lost someone, someone who has felt the pain, and someone who was helped by a funeral director like me. To them...I'm a regular person...providing an extraordinary service...and that makes it all worthwhile. I'm Bill Johnston, and I am a Funeral Director at Johnston Funeral Home and Crematory, Baldwin County's oldest, family-owned funeral home."*

What is a traditional funeral? You know what a traditional funeral is, but maybe the consumer doesn't, and wouldn't you love to have more traditional funerals? Explain it! Educate the consumer. You believe there's a benefit. Share that feeling with them. You can talk about the funeral process, from the benefit of being with a loved one for the last time, the feeling families get when they surround them and say their goodbyes, and even how a burial gives everyone a perpetual place to make that physical connection with the deceased. This fits The Premier, Emerging, and Plateaued Funeral Homes, and the Buyer Types are At-Need and The Preplanner.

Here's a Facebook post that speaks to this: *"Seeing a loved one for the last time is a deep human need and a revered funeral tradition. It not only confirms their transition, but it is also known to ease the grieving process. To learn more about traditional funerals, call Johnston Funeral Home, 919-223-8988, and meet with a Funeral Director like Bill Johnston."*

Did you know consumers considering cremation have options? This is a significant topic because no single trend is threatening cash flow greater than cremation, and to be specific, direct cremation. What the public does not know is *why* funerals have been done in a certain way. And although grieving is a highly individual experience, grief counselors believe viewing the deceased plays a crucial role in the grieving process. It helps surviving family members confront the reality of loss and begin the journey towards acceptance and closure. Messaging can include the need for a private viewing, a body present for a visitation or celebration of life, even embalming and viewing as a lasting memory known as a "traditional cremation." Funeral Home Types will be The Premier, Emerging, Innovator, and Specialty. Buyer types include The Immediate Buyer (personas including Loyal, Second Timer, Caring, and Faith or Cultural Buyer), The Preplanner (all personas except The Authoritative Planner), and The Customizer.

Here's a 60-second radio ad that speaks to this: *"Have you recently been to a funeral? This is Bill johnston, a Funeral Director for Johnston Funeral Home and Crematory. If you've recently been to a visitation or celebration of life, have you wondered why things are done in a certain way? At Johnston Funeral Home and Crematory, families ask us to fulfill their time-honored traditions. And you may not realize it, but funerals are for the living. It gives them the emotional foundation they need to heal and discover hope. It's when a family chooses cremation, they might forget the options of a visitation or celebration of life, and then after the fact, realize something's missing. That's why at Johnston Funeral Home and Crematory, we offer the option of a Traditional Cremation. It's just like a Traditional Funeral, except there is no graveside service. To learn about the Traditional Cremation, call us, or come see us, at Johnston Funeral Home and Crematory, Baldwin County's oldest family-owned funeral home."*

Does a funeral have to be expensive? This topic can educate consumers on how to celebrate a life while respecting budgets, wishes, or needs. Being transparent on pricing can empower consumers to make informed decisions that align with their financial and emotional needs. This is a topic for The Price Strategy Funeral Home educating the Price Sensitive buyer, but also The Innovator Funeral Home if it strives to fulfill diverse needs and preferences.

Here's a Facebook post that speaks to the topic called value: "A celebration of life will be a memory that lasts forever. That's why families who need to save yet want the finest call Johnston Funeral Home. From pricing to the beauty of our facility, we strive to offer the best funeral value. For more, call 919-223-8988."

What kind of funeral creates the smallest footprint on the environment? According to a joint study from McKensey and

NielsenIQ, 78 percent of US consumers say a sustainable lifestyle is important to them (Jordan Bar Am, February 6, 2023). That's a big number, and even though not everyone makes purchases based on sustainability, it will be a growing trend as Baby Boomers are replaced by Generation X. Funeral Home Types include The Innovator and Price Strategy. Buyer types include The Price Sensitive buyer (minimalist) and The Customizer (eco-conscious buyer).

Here's a Facebook post that speaks to this topic: *"Simplicity and sustainability. That's at the core of every green burial. By being placed in a biodegradable container, and being interred in a grave to decompose fully, a life can return to nature. To learn more, call Johnston Funeral Home, 919-223-8988."*

How can you make a funeral extraordinary? Alan J. MacKinnon, CCE, President and General Manager of The Gardens Cemetery in Boston, is an advocate for ceremonies, and one of his is called, "The Extraordinary Funeral." It's described as a funeral type where, "you will be freed from traditional constraints so the entire event can be completely personalized." The Extraordinary Funeral can be led by a Certified Celebrant or funeral professional and lets a consumer "create anything you can imagine, something new and meaningful." Where it's held can be unique, food can be served, live music performed, whatever can be imagined. Funeral Home Type would be The Innovator. Buyer types could be The Preplanner (Storyteller) and The Customizer (The Celebrator).

Here's a Facebook post that speaks to this topic: *"With an extraordinary funeral, you will be freed from traditional constraints so the entire event can be completely personalized. It's how you, your friends, and your family want to say a final goodbye to someone you love. For help creating an Extraordinary Funeral, let's listen to your needs and discover which funeral home, celebrant, or funeral advisor may be the best fit for you and your family. For an appointment, call The Gardens Cemetery, (617) 325-0186."*

Does a funeral have to be a religious experience? According to Pew Research, secular shifts in society show no signs of slowing. The report reveals that roughly three in ten US adults are now religiously unaffiliated or "nones" (people who describe themselves as atheists, or "nothing in particular" when asked about their religious identity) (Smith, December 14, 2021). As this demographic shift continues, with it comes increased demand for non-religious or secular funeral options. Funeral Home Types would be The Innovator and The Specialty funeral homes and goes across all Funeral Buyer Types.

What are the legal and practical considerations when preparing for the loss of a loved one? Attorneys and financial planners are active participants on this topic, but it also makes sense for funeral homes to connect customers with trusted professionals who can answer questions. This fits The Premier, Emerging, and Innovator Funeral Homes focusing on The Preplanner buyer type (personas are the planner and the financial planner).

"Did You Figure it Out?"

If you are clear about your Funeral Home Type (you know who you are and you know what you stand for), and the ideal Funeral Buyers you want to attract, then did you see examples of education that would fit your firm? How to match thinking patterns? Or better yet, did you receive an inspiration on an educational topic that's not one of these 10? Your takeaway from this chapter should be that you can educate consumers as a strategy to build trust with them so that, when they enter Phase 3 – Desire, you are the only and obvious choice.

Key Thoughts from Chapter 18:

1. Education is a preferred form of forward motion for funeral homes.

2. A Funeral Buyer Type and persona is a consumer's "thinking pattern."

3. The Funeral Home Types are The Premier, The Emerging, The Innovator, The Price Strategy, The Specialty, and The Plateaued Funeral Homes.

4. Matching your Funeral Home Type with your ideal Buyer Types and their "thinking patterns" will make it easier to create educational topics they would be interested in. See Reference 2, Campaign Worksheet.

5. By providing clear, helpful, trust-building education in Phases 1 and 2 of the Consumer's Journey, consumers may feel more confident and secure, then they enter Phase 4 and decide your funeral home is the only and obvious choice.

CHAPTER NINETEEN

How to Feel Good About Sales

The roadmap has been defined. From Chapter 12, How to Grow a Business, to Chapter 18, Educating the Consumer, you have my best effort. It's a place to start, and like any other map you need one if you know where you're going. It contains the keys to making your market share and revenue grow with marketing and advertising.

In this chapter, which is my riff, I want to share some thoughts on growing revenue. It's called sales. If you're successful, if you bring new consumers to your funeral home, how do you intend to increase the amount of money they give you for the services you are willing to render? Chapter 12, How to Grow a Business, is worth reading again. It describes the four ways (and there are only four) to grow your business. It should get you thinking about your sales process, what happens when a consumer clicks a link on a website, calls a phone number, or walks through your door.

Full Disclosure Again

As you know, I have never worked at a funeral home, although for one day when I was 18 I transported flowers for a funeral home in my hometown to a graveside. So this chapter is not coming to you from an expert in the funeral sales process, but it is coming to you from someone who is an expert in sales. My resume begins with direct, home-improvement sales (two years, 60% close rate, sold to every consumer type you can imagine), spans 25 years of media sales in broadcasting; I was a national leader in mortgage technology enterprise sales while mastering the complex sales process for 10 years; I sold and produced national tv ads and interactive media to the largest cable television providers in the US; and, you're reading my book. That's a sale, too.

What I see for you is an opportunity. By reaching Ideal Consumers, by following them through the Funeral Sales Funnel, and investing time, effort, and resources on increasing traffic to your funeral home, can you change the way you sell them when they arrive to purchase or to preplan? Remember, the change you make may not have to be so big. You may not have to break everything. Here are some facts for you to consider:

1. Who knows more about what the consumer needs to solve their funeral problem? Someone who has never purchased a funeral before, or a funeral professional or someone like you who has seen and heard hundreds or thousands of families experience a funeral? A funeral professional who knows what's best, who knows the long-term benefits of doing a funeral a certain way, the right way? A funeral professional who has seen first-hand what it takes to make a family happy? The answer is the funeral director. The funeral director knows best. That makes the funeral director an expert.

2. Are all funeral directors sales professionals? No.

3. Do all funeral directors believe that "sales" is a good thing? No.

4. Do all funeral directors, owners, and operators believe sales is a positive word? No.

5. Do all funeral home owners and operators believe in maximizing sales? No.

6. Do all funeral home owners and operators have ongoing training programs to help funeral directors sell more? No.

7. Would all funeral home owners and operators like to see the average sale amount for a funeral grow? YES. ABSOLUTELY.

"Sales is the Transference of a Feeling" – Zig Ziglar

If your funeral home does 100 cases a year, and you grew each case by $500, and in the process of doing it, your funeral directors feel good about doing it, and the families you serve feel good about the services they received, wouldn't you feel good about it, too? Wouldn't it be worth trying? Just think about it. 100 x $500 is $50,000. That's either $50,000 that could be used for you to take a vacation, pay yourself more, or invest in the beauty of your funeral home. And if you're doing 200 calls, it's $100,000. What could you do with an extra $100,000? That would feel good. Wouldn't it? So here are three thoughts, observations, or ideas (I don't know what to call them but they're solid) to help you feel good about the value of adding sales to your sales process:

1. Who knows how much money the consumer can spend on a funeral? Answer: The Consumer. The funeral director does not, but funeral directors who believe cost is foremost on the consumer's mind think they do. Their point of view is to help the consumer save. But what if the consumer is not interested in saving? Does a consumer walk out of an arrangement meeting and pat themselves on the back because they saved a few bucks? No. Let the consumer decide how much they can spend. THEY KNOW HOW MUCH THEY HAVE. The funeral director does not. Sure, you have a price list and there are rules, but consider this: The first thing you offer, whether it is for a traditional funeral or cremation, let it be the BIGGEST service you offer. Sales rule: When you offer prices, you can always come down, but you can never go up. You may be *surprised* by what the consumer does. They may choose the biggest and the best. And if they did, and they received the biggest and best, would they walk away months later and say that they paid too much? Pumped because they saved a few bucks? Probably not. Probably...they will feel good about what they purchased because it felt good, it felt right, and will feel right forever.

2. As casket sales are trending down, there is a growing trend to sell merchandise. But what are you really selling? This is a conversation about what is tangible and what is not. As a broadcaster, my product, what we made and sold, was intangible. Radio. So because you can't touch it or feel it, does that mean it's worth less? NO. But some people who sell funeral services may not feel there is a cost or value associated with something that is intangible, so they don't value it. They value a casket because there is a cost. They value an urn because there is a cost. I guess

there is a cost of electricity in cremation (forget the fact you paid $200,000 for the machine), but not much more. Right? WRONG. The services a funeral home provides are incredibly valuable. Most funeral homes consider their reputation to be their most valuable asset. That's intangible, too. Raise the prices of your services and feel good about it.

3. When price is the issue, it is the only issue. There's a reason Price Strategy Funeral Homes advertise a certain way. They lead with price. They are attracting consumers who want the best price. But if you're not a Price Strategy Funeral Home, go back and read item 1 in my riff. Anecdotally, in sales, I have suggested that only 10% of consumers purchase what they purchase strictly on price. Nobody has ever disagreed with me. Ever.

I could go on. Yes, it's a riff. But this chapter alone could change your business.

Key Thoughts from Chapter 19:

1. Revenue is also called sales. If you think that I consider sales to be a positive word, you're right.

2. Who knows more about what a consumer needs to solve their funeral problem? A funeral director.

3. Sales can be defined as a transference of a feeling.

4. Making an extra $500 per call will feel good.

5. When price is the issue, it is the only issue.

6. I could go on.

CHAPTER

Gratitude and Next Steps

If you're reading this chapter, thank you. In writing this book, I have attempted to arrange a wide variety of very diverse ideas and concepts and organize them so that they are logical and practical. I hope that your expectations have been exceeded.

Throughout the book I repeated a few phrases, one of which was, "Do you know who you are and you know what you stand for." What's remarkable to me is not everyone knows who they are and what they stand for. They let the work and their life get in front of their ability to think clearly and use their mind to imagine what they want. If that's you, then I hope this book changes your perspective and helps you get back on track. It's a thought starter, and I wrote it to get you to think.

In Reference 2 that follows, Helpful Worksheets, I'm pointing you to my website where you can download a worksheet called, "Do you know who you are, and do you know what you stand for?" that includes a way to look at the competitive landscape. Reference 2 also lists a few more supporting worksheets that will bring your marketing and advertising efforts to life.

You know by now I use repetition as a part of my writing style to make it easier to remember key thoughts. So...to repeat, this is my intended result for you. That if you read this book, take action, and then we meet at a trade show or online, you could declare that you are:

"Professionally, consistently, and effectively marketing to Ideal Consumers in a certain way for the purpose of establishing an equity position in their mind, so that when they consciously decide to purchase funeral services, your firm is top of mind, making it the only and obvious choice."

If I can be of benefit to you, or help you figure out how to get from where you are to where you want to be, visit my website: www.postandboost.com. Make an appointment with me. Let me get to know you. You can also call me, 336-516-9163. Together we can help you develop your roadmap to grow your market share and revenue.

Reference 1
The "On Phenomenon"

The "On Phenomenon" describes how a consumer's mind works, and how it has two spheres, the "conscious" and the "subconscious" spheres. The conscious can only think about one thing at a time. It's incredibly powerful but easily forgets. On the other hand, the subconscious remembers everything like a filing cabinet. Sigmund Freud, in the book, *The Interpretation of Dreams*, writes, "Nothing can be brought to an end in the unconscious; nothing is past or forgotten" (Freud, 1950).

The "On Phenomenon" is based on the Baader-Meinhof Phenomenon, and "Why do we keep noticing certain things more often?" (Henderson, 2023). This phenomenon, also known as the frequency illusion, is highlighted in discussions around patterns of recognition. For example, purchasing a red Jeep might suddenly make you notice red Jeeps everywhere. This pattern recognition, where "whatever you focus on, you'll find," underscores the workings of the subconscious mind.

The Baader-Meinhof Phenomenon has a strong connection to the working of the subconscious mind. In essence, it illustrates how the subconscious mind filters and prioritizes information.

When applied to marketing and advertising and how it relates to the consumer's journey, the concept can be described as the "On Phenomenon." Here, a consumer's preoccupation with thoughts of mortality or the loss of a loved one makes them receptive or "On" to funeral home advertising. It's not that these ads are happening more frequently, but rather the consumer's subconscious mind is actively seeking them out.

Reference 2
Powerful Worksheets

If you visit this page on my website, PostandBoost.com/worksheets, you'll be able to download these helpful worksheets:

- <u>Do you know who you are, and do you know what you stand for</u>? This will help you answer the questions we have asked throughout the book. This also helps you better define the competitive landscape.

- <u>Defining your Ideal Consumers using their thinking patterns</u>. This helps you narrow down the desired Funeral Buyer Types you want to attract to your funeral home based on your Funeral Home Type.

- <u>How to calculate the number of consumers you need to reach to achieve a growth objective</u>. This is designed to help you define your "smallest viable market."

- <u>Creating a campaign</u>. Using the four Growth Strategies as a starting point, this worksheet will help you conceptualize a campaign including budgeting, media, and messaging.

Acknowledgements

I've done my best to combine my knowledge and experience in the funeral industry with my marketing and advertising background. Who helped me along the way, gave me knowledge and wisdom, and the skills to write this book are many. I'm going to try to recognize them here.

Many thanks to some of my first funeral home customers. To name a few who had the patience to answer my questions and give me knowledge, they are Ven Faulk, Paula and Jim Lowe, Jack and Dan Briggs, Neil Fair, Staton Carter, Jeff Nobles, Mickey Pore, Kelly Clements, Joe Trippodo III, JB Rhodes III, Les Powell, and Paul Phillips. I also want to thank Charlie Evans, Bob Groves, Casey Lynch, Matthew Jernigan, Brian Bowser, Jay Wilkinson, The Real Tom Jones, Alan Creedy, Matthew Ayer, Andy Huffine, Ann Wiliams, Barry Theriot, Doug Huggins, Richard Diehl, JimmiAnne Lowe, Eric Rudd, Neil Roberts, Dwayne Josey, John Vogler, C'Archer Small, and Alan MacKinnon for helping me with my book and industry knowledge.

In the marketing and advertising world, thank you to Seth Godin for allowing me to borrow some of his words, Don Curtis for how advertising works, and mastermind partner Diana Needham for this book concept.

In the funeral industry, thank you to Sara Moss of NFDA, and that organization's invitation to speak on this book at their 2024 International Convention and Expo in New Orleans.

AND...my awesome family, Cecelia, Jennifer, Matt, Phill, Hudson, Wes, Max, Cecelia, and Will.

About the Author

Bill A Johnston is an Advertising and Facebook Expert for Funeral Homes, President of Post and Boost (an advertising agency), speaker, author of four books including "How Facebook Works for Funeral Homes," and a Meta Business Partner. A native of Jamestown NY, Bill graduated from the Newhouse School at Syracuse University with a degree in Television and Radio in 1977 and has 25 years of experience managing radio stations in the Carolinas.

In 2000 he founded iconnectv.com, an interactive media company for cable television. He produced national television commercials for Charter Communications and interactive lead generating platforms including the Answers! Interactive CD for Cox Communications, and The Time Warner Cable Business Analyzer.

In 2016 he became a Facebook expert, invented a proprietary, scalable software platform that creates, posts, and boosts custom advertising for Funeral Homes on Facebook, and is dedicated to inspiring funeral home owners and operators to discover advertising can work for funeral homes.

Bill is also a talented speaker and has appeared before numerous national and state associations. He is a Certified Provider with the Academy of Professional Funeral Service Practice, as well as a CE provider to multiple state funeral boards. He's married to his wife of 45 years, Cecelia, has two children, a son-in-law, and five grandchildren. He lives in Daphne, Alabama.

Bibliography

Broadcasters, N. A. (2024, January 4). *Study Finds TV and Radio Broadcasters Significant Contributors to Nations Economy*. Retrieved from nab.org: https://www.nab.org/documents/newsroom/pressRelease.asp?id=6911

Corbett, M. (1999). *The 33 Ruthless Rules of Local Advertising*. New York, New York: SummitView Publishing.

Elisabeth Kubler-Ross, M. (1969). *On Death & Dying*. New York, NY: Scribner, An Imprint of Simon & Schuster, Inc.

Farida B. Ahmas, M., Jodi A. Cisewski, M., Jiaquan Xu, M., & Robert N. Anderson, P. (2023, May 5). *Morbidity and Mortality Weekly Report*. Retrieved from Centers for Disease Control and Prevention: https://www.cdc.gov/mmwr/volumes/72/wr/mm7218a3.htm

Freud, S. (1950). *The Interpretation of Dreams*. New York: Random House, Inc.

Godin, S. (1999). *Godin, Seth. "Permission Marketing." Turning Strangers Into Friends And Friends Into Customers, Simon and Schuster, 1999, https://doi.org/10.1604/9780684856360*. Retrieved from Wikipedia.

Godin, S. (2018). This Is Marketing. You can't be Seen Until You Learn to See. (Portfolio/Penguin)

Henderson, S. (2023). *Baader-Meinhof Phenomenon: Why do we keep noticing certain things more often?* Kindle.

Hugh Wilson, R. S. (1979, March 26). *IMDb*. Retrieved from WKRP in Cincinnati Commercial Break: https://www.imdb. com/title/tt0742601/

Jordan Bar Am, V. D. (February 6, 2023). Consumers care about sustainability - and back it up with their wallets. *McKinsey & Company*, https://www.mckinsey.com/industries/ consumer-packaged-goods/our-insights/consumers-care-about-sustainability-and-back-it-up-with-their-wallets.

Lackey, C. A. (Unknown). Furniture Sales and Funeral Homes. *Hilldsale County Historical Society*. Retrieved from https:// www.hillsdalehistoricalsociety.org/furniture-sales-and-funeral-homes

Lovecraft, H. (2020). *Supernatural Horror in Literature*. Prabhat Prakashan.

Lynn Hasher, D. G. (1977). *Frequency and the Conference of Referential Validity*.

Murphy, D. J. (1963). *The Power of Your Subconscious Mind*. Prentice Hall Press.

Neilsberg. (2023, September 17). *United States Population by Age*. Retrieved from Neilsberg: https://www.neilsberg. com/insights/united-states-population-by-age/

Schaeffer, K. (2024, February 2). *pewresearch.org*. Retrieved from Pew Research Center: https://www.pewresearch. org/short-reads/2024/02/02/5-facts-about-how-americans-use-facebook-two-decades-after-its-launch/

Simpson, J. (2017). *Finding Brand Success in the Digital World*. Forbes. Retrieved from https://www.forbes.com/sites/

forbesagencycouncil/2017/08/25/finding-brand-suc-
cess-in-the-digital-world/?sh=6807ea5d626e

Smith, G. A. (December 14, 2021). About Three-in-Ten U.S. Adults
Are Now Religiously Unaffiliated. *Pew Research Center*,
https://www.pewresearch.org/religion/2021/12/14/
about-three-in-ten-u-s-adults-are-now-religiously-unaf-
filiated/#:~:text=Currently%2C%20about%20three-in-
ten%20U.S.%20adults%20%2829%25%29%20are%2-
0religious,in%20particular%E2%80%9D%20when%20
asked%20about%20t.

Trout, R. a. (2001). Positioning: The Battle For Your Mind. In J. T.
Al Ries, *Positioning: The Battle For Your Mind.* McGraw-Hill.

Wattles, W. (1910). *The Science of Getting Rich.* Holyoke, Mass.:
The Elizabeth Towne Company.

Wilks, C. (2023, June 22). *A Content Creator's Best Friend.* Retrieved
from Psychology Today: https://www.psychologytoday.
com/us/blog/human-flourishing-101/202306/a-con-
tent-creators-best-friend

Made in the USA
Columbia, SC
05 August 2024

39608068R00093